NORTHAMPTONSHIRE AT WAR 1939–45

1. The Duchess of Gloucester (now Princess Alice, Duchess of Gloucester) visits the Northamptonshire Institute of Agriculture at Moulton on 28th March 1941. On her right is Countess Spencer, County Chairman of the Women's Land Army.

NORTHAMPTONSHIRE AT WAR 1939–45

A selection of photographs

Northamptonshire Libraries

1978

Published by
NORTHAMPTONSHIRE LIBRARIES
27 Guildhall Road, Northampton NN1 1EF

ISBN 0-905391-04-7

Designed by Bernard Crossland Associates
Type set in Monotype Baskerville 169 11/12 pt.
and printed in Great Britain by
Cheney & Sons Ltd., Banbury, Oxon.

ACKNOWLEDGEMENTS

Northamptonshire Libraries wish to thank the following individuals, firms and organisations for permission to reproduce their photographs: Her Royal Highness Princess Alice, Duchess of Gloucester (199, 200); The Marquis of Northampton (227-9); Mr. and Mrs. E. R. Barker (2, 5, 6); Mr. F. W. Barker (55-6); Bassett-Lowke, Ltd. (135-6); Mr. N. R. Bazeley (183); Mr. B. E. Billington (37, 46); Mr. L. Black (42, 74); Mr. Quentin Bland (257-8, 260, 273-4); Mr. G. J. Boothroyd (248, 251); Mrs. J. E. Brassington (193); British Red Cross Society (47); British Steel Corporation (133-4); British Timken (129); Brooklands Aviation, Ltd. (138-40, 142); Chapman & Hall, Ltd. (21); Charter Trustees of the Town of Daventry (178); Chief Constable of Northamptonshire (51, 63, 83); Mr. H. Clifton (73); College of Agriculture, Moulton (110-112, 114); Mrs. M. Coyne (106); Mrs. R. Dixon (31); Express Lift Co., Ltd. (80, 123-6); Fox Photos, Ltd. (1); Mr. G. Freeston (36); Mr. R. D. Frey (100); Mr. A. J. George (38, 287, 291); Mr. M. L. Gibson (92, 192, 197, 232, 245, 249, 256, 259, 267, 270-2, 280-1, and information for 282); Chief Inspector G. Hall (89); Mr. Roland Holloway (3-4, 7, 10-20, 22-5, 27-8, 32-5, 39-41, 43-5, 48, 52-4, 60-2, 66-7, 75-7, 81, 90-1, 93-9, 102-3, 109, 113, 115, 132, 144, 147, 149-52, 156, 162-3, 165-6, 170-6, 181, 191, 194-6, 215-7, 219-24, 226, 230-1, 283-5, 233-5, 292); Imperial War Museum, Department of Art (30, 160-1, 168-9); Imperial War Museum, Department of Photographs (237-44, 246-7, 250, 252-3, 255); Keesing's Contemporary Archives (159); Kettering Library (146); Mr. R. J. Kitchin (122a); Mrs. T. C. A. Knight (198); Mr. G. S. Lewis (131, 186); Mr. H. C. W. Lewis (211-14); Mr. P. E. Lewis (148, 153-5, 157, 201-10); Mr. A. J. Linnell (137, 158, 290); Mr. R. A. Ludgate (254); Mr. J. Mackaness (104-5, 107-8, 119); Mr. H. Masters (164); Mrs. L. G. Norman (190); Northampton Mercury Co., Ltd. (113); Northampton Museums (289); Northamptonshire County Record Office (65, 68-72, 82, 84-8, 188); Northamptonshire Evening Telegraph (26, 182); Northamptonshire Federation of Women's Institutes (177); Northamptonshire Regiment (236); Mrs. H. B. Parkinson (116-17, 120); Mr. K. C. Peasgood (49); Mrs. E. W. Piggott (57-9, 127, 288); Mr. C. Putt (50, 167); St. Andrews University (64); Mr. R. Sismey (225, 261-6, 268, 275-9); Mr. P. Stafford (79); Mr. R. Stewart (269), Mr. H. Taylor, O.B.E. (130); Mr. J. H. Thornton (8-9, 29, 122, 145, 179-80, 286); Mr. T. H. Turney (118); Mr. Lou Warwick (184-5, 187, 189); Mr. R. Warwick (121); Miss W. Wharton (101); Charles Wicksteed, Ltd. (128); Mr. F. A. Wright (141, 143); Mrs. N. E. Wright (218).

Acknowledgement is made to those owners of copyright who have permitted the reproduction of photographs: Mrs. Eric Ager (items 199, 227-9); The Northampton Mercury Co. Ltd. (a total of 104 photographs); the United States Air Force (items 225, 256-65, 267-73, 275-81); The Northamptonshire Evening Telegraph (items 26, 101, 182); Central Office of Information, previously Ministry of Information (items 110-12).

Valuable help in compiling the text has been provided by the following: Mr. Roland Holloway, previously photographer with the Northampton Mercury Co. Ltd., whose magnificent collection of photographs forms the basis of this book; Mr. R. A. Barber (agriculture); Major D. Baxter (Northamptonshire Regiment); Dr. J. S. Blair ('Pluto'); Mr. Quentin Bland (Grafton Underwood air base); Mr. T. H. Cockerill (air raid shelters); Mr. M. L. Gibson (Air Force history and details of airfields); Mr. G. A. Jelley (Northamptonshire Yeomanry); Mr. R. J. Kitchin (boot and shoe industry); Mr. H. M. Newton (aircraft assembly); Mr. P. E. Lewis (family history); Mr. F. W. Nicholas (aircraft repair); Mr. T. Park (Moulton Institute of Agriculture); Mrs. H. B. Parkinson (Women's Land Army); Mr. Desmond Perkins (industry); Mr. R. Sismey (Deenethorpe air base); Mr. H. J. Smith (aircraft repair and assembly); Miss J. Swann M.B.E. (boot and shoe industry); Mr. S. H. Swannell (emergency services); Mr. J. H. Thornton (boot and shoe industry); Mr. Lou Warwick (theatre); Mr. R. Warwick (prisoners of war); Mr. F. A. Wright (aircraft repair). The section on agriculture has been based upon Mr. T. H. Turney's pamphlet *War-time farming in Northamptonshire.* Northamptonshire Libraries also wish to thank Mr. H. J. Mann, Mr. A. C. Watts, and Mr. A. C. Whiting for allowing their family snapshots to be reproduced. Original photographic work has been undertaken by Beedle and Cooper, Northampton.

CONTENTS

INTRODUCTION

The purpose of this book is to provide a pictorial record of Northamptonshire's contribution to the Second World War. Such a period is difficult to depict due to the scarcity of film at the time, and the degree of secrecy which surrounded those activities which were directly concerned with the war effort, such as the manufacture of aircraft, ammunition, etc. Also, since the war many families have discarded personal documents and photographs which would otherwise have formed a valuable link with the past. Despite this, a public appeal made by Northamptonshire Libraries in January 1978 did bring to light several hundred photographs, and a number of these appear in the book. The co-operation and knowledge of many Northamptonshire people have also been of immense value in compiling the captions accompanying the illustrations. In some cases original records have either been lost or deliberately destroyed, and here the text relies upon the memories of those involved at the time. It has become clear in compiling the book that every section deserves much more detailed study than is possible in a short pictorial survey, and we can only apologise to those who find their own particular interest inadequately represented or absent.

Photographs can give a distorted view of events, as they often show people 'making the best of things'; nevertheless, it is hoped that this collection will be successful in illustrating the skills, dedication and courage shown in the fight for survival of a free society.

Throughout the book individuals are given the titles and decorations obtaining at the time—only in exceptional cases are references made to post-war honours or positions.

PREPARATIONS FOR WAR

AIR RAID SHELTERS

2. Trench digging on Northampton 'Racecourse', 1st October 1938. The Munich crisis of September, 1938, impressed upon both government and population the necessity for speeding contingency plans in the event of the outbreak of war, and the expected enemy air raids. On 24th September the Home Office asked local authorities of all densely populated areas to give the highest priority to digging trenches. The purpose of this was to enable those members of the public caught in the open during an air raid to find shelter. They were later extended and strengthened to form substantial underground shelters.

3. Work on one of the five underground shelters on Northampton's 'Racecourse', much of which was put to military use. 'Talavera Camp' was built there to accommodate in turn a basic training unit and a training centre for A.T.S. At the end of the war a major demobilisation centre was set up here. Eventually the 'Racecourse' was returned to its original state at the insistence of the County Borough.

4. The entrance to the underground shelter on Dallington Park, Northampton.

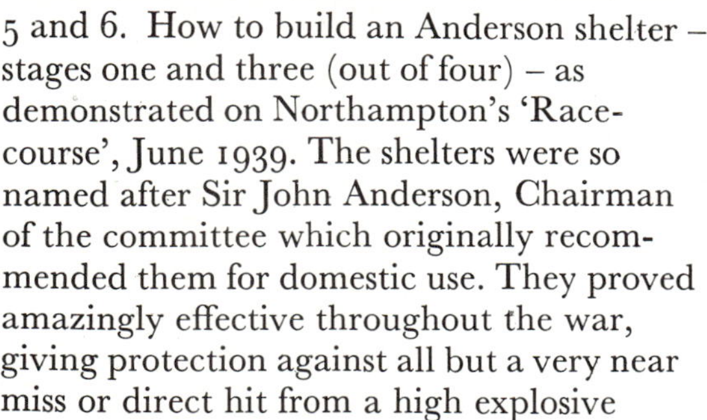
5 and 6. How to build an Anderson shelter – stages one and three (out of four) – as demonstrated on Northampton's 'Racecourse', June 1939. The shelters were so named after Sir John Anderson, Chairman of the committee which originally recommended them for domestic use. They proved amazingly effective throughout the war, giving protection against all but a very near miss or direct hit from a high explosive bomb. Their one major defect was a tendency to flood. By April 1939 nearly 300,000, protecting an estimated 1½ million people, had been delivered; by the outbreak of war 1½ million had been distributed. Intended to protect four people, they could accommodate six if necessary. They were free to households with an income of not more than £250 per annum.

7. A completed Anderson shelter with inhabitants Barbara and Jacqueline Gardner of 5 Addison Road, Northampton, May 1940. In most towns householders were responsible for their erection, which sometimes led to delays. In Corby by April 1940 only 50% of those issued had been installed.

8 and 9. Some families joined together to build their own shelters. This one at 41 The Headlands, Northampton, served four households.

10. This photograph of a shelter being subjected to a test weight of eight tons was published in August 1940. By autumn the unsatisfactory state of Northampton's surface shelters had become apparent.

11. Surface shelters being built in Herbert Street, Northampton. In April 1940 the severe shortage of steel caused the government to cancel all further orders for Anderson shelters. From then onwards the emphasis was on brick built communal street shelters above ground, each accommodating about fifty people. Unfortunately an ambiguously worded memorandum issued by the central Air Raid Precautions Department persuaded many local authorities that a suitable mortar for use in such shelters could be made from lime and sand with no cement. The result was that throughout the country shelters collapsed from the effects of inclement weather rather than enemy action.

12. Union Street, Northampton.

The effects of rainy weather on surface shelters. These photographs were not passed for publication at the time. In Northampton 950 shelters had to be reconstructed out of an original 1,255; 534 had been completed by June 1941. On the second occasion the mortar used was so strong that when the shelters were demolished in 1946 the bricks, not the mortar, broke and could not be re-used for other building purposes.

13. London Road Northampton.

14. Essex Street, Northampton.

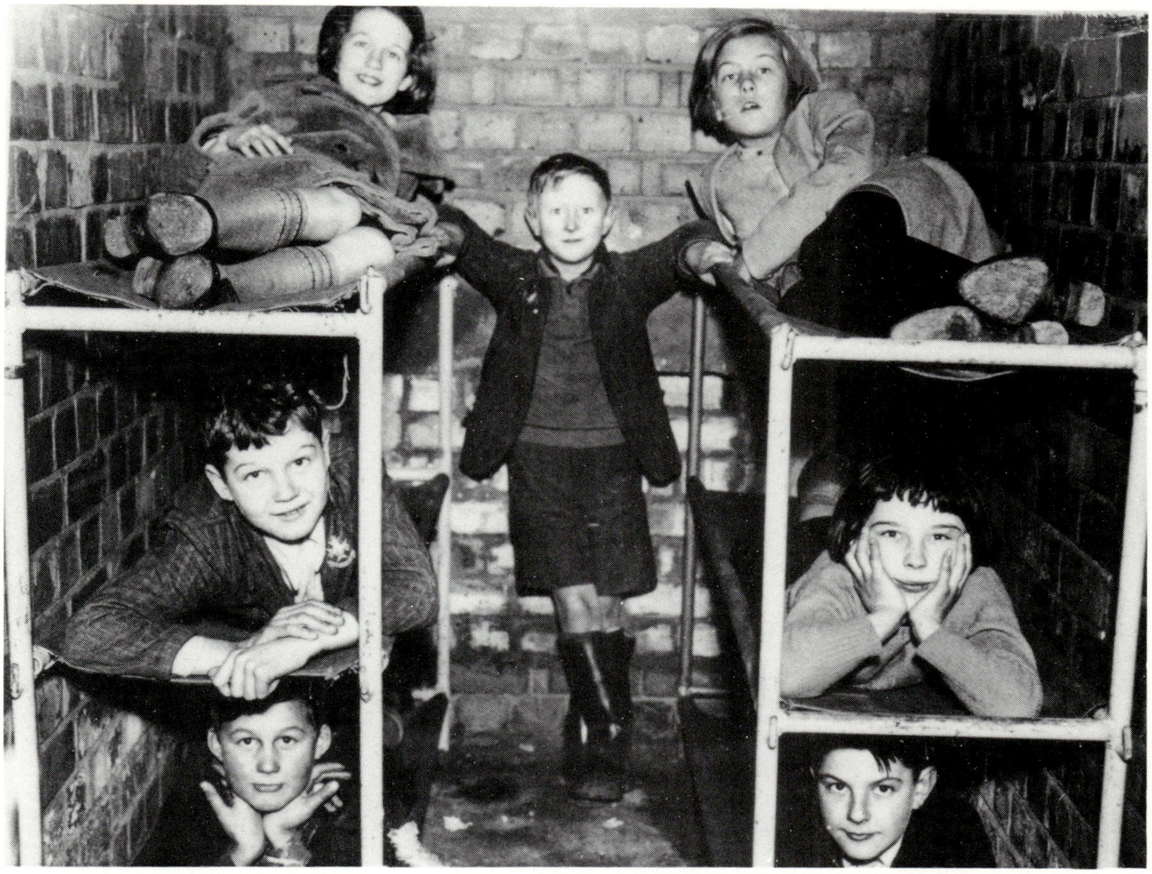

The shelters in Thingummy Road

Bricks on the road in a puddle,
 Some sand and a little red light,
All that remains of the muddle,
 Whom do these things indict?

Asked if the shelters were needed,
 We answered, 'No, not here.'
We said – and it wasn't heeded –
Each house had a cellar, t'was clear.

But up came the road in a flurry,
 More slowly they builded the walls;
Then flung on the roofs in a hurry –
 Then followed the premature falls.

There came the wintry weather,
 The rain, the snow and the frost,
The shelters all crumbled together,
 And that's how the money is lost.

'Seafell'

Chronicle and Echo, 31st January 1941

15. Northampton children test out shelters under the Market Square. They were not in fact used, as they would not have stood up to a direct hit.

16. Entrance to an underground shelter in The Drapery, Northampton.

SANDBAGS

The protection of public buildings against bomb blast was given a high priority by the government, and by the start of 1939 24 million sandbags had been distributed, and a further 275 million ordered.

17. Northampton Guildhall entrance, September 1939. By January 1940 there was criticism in the local press about the speed with which sandbags had rotted; it was claimed that they had become a sanctuary for rats.

18. Sandbags being mechanically filled at West Bridge Depot, Northampton, August 1939. The method was invented by Northampton's Borough Engineer, R. A. Winfield.

19. The General Hospital, Northampton, September 1939.

DEFENCE AGAINST POISON GAS

During the 1930s there was the fear that any enemy which attacked this country would make use of poison gas. This was based upon the fact that gas had been used fairly extensively in the first world war on the western front, and had again been used by Italy in its campaign against Abyssinia in 1936. As early as January 1938 twenty five million gas masks had been accumulated, and many were already distributed by the Munich crisis in September.

20. Children try on their gas masks, December 1939.

21. The Siebe-Gorman anti-gas hood for babies. The hood was made of rubberised fabric, the window of cellulose acetate. Air was pumped in through a filter by working the bellows to their full extent up and down forty times per minute. There was also a special gas bag available for smaller babies.

22. A gas mask store in Northampton.

23. Gas mask practice in the jobbing room of the *Chronicle and Echo*.

24. Gas mask drill at the telephone exchange, Northampton, September 1939.

25. Testing gas masks at the Fire Station, The Mounts, Northampton.

EVACUEES

The government anticipated massive air attacks upon the major urban areas of Britain immediately war was declared, and with this in mind contingency plans were made for the evacuation of children. Children in vulnerable areas were either privately evacuated to friends or relatives in safe areas, or were 'officially' evacuated with the school. In the former case children were sometimes accompanied by their mothers. Between June 1939 and the first week in September over 3½ million are estimated to have moved from high risk to less vulnerable areas. Of these 2 million evacuated themselves privately to friends or relatives; 1½ million were decanted briskly into the countryside between 1st and 3rd September. Northamptonshire, being a low risk area, was designated a 'wholly reception county'. By September 1939 it had accommodated 42,529 evacuees, a number exceeded only by one other county, Somerset (46,532).

26. Disconsolate evacuees arrive at Kettering. 'The majority of Kettering's new population consists of members of working class families from London suburbs. Girls from convent and secondary schools are also included. There are, too, quite a number of coloured boys and girls.' *Mercury and Herald*, 8th September 1939.

27. Evacuees receive refreshments at Cedar Road School reception centre, Northampton. During the hectic days of the official evacuation 5th and 6th form students from local schools helped man reception centres.

28. Evacuated schoolteachers arrive in Northampton carrying their gas masks.

29. School meals in the canteen of the Rushden Boot and Shoe School 1942, where children from St. Pancras Primary School, London, had been evacuated.

30. Despite posters such as this, by January 1940 900,000 evacuees had returned to the target areas; in June 1940, Kettering reported that only 1,887 evacuees remained out of the original 5,000; by September four fifths of Northampton's 15,000 had returned home.

31. Village children and evacuees at Aldwincle support War Weapons Week, May 10-17, 1941.

32. These children were Polish and German refugees; originally evacuated to Chamberlayne Road School, Willesden, they found temporary refuge at Rothersthorpe Road School, Far Cotton. On the right is their teacher, Mr. D. Clitheroe, September 1939.

EMERGENCY SERVICES

The civil defence services of England, Scotland and Wales were divided into 12 regions, and Northamptonshire was included in the North Midlands region (no. 3) with its headquarters and Regional Commissioner based at Nottingham. Although there was close liaison, the County and County Borough had independent organisations, each controlled by an Emergency Committee which was set up following a Home Office instruction on 31st August 1939.

The County's Emergency Committee took over from the Air Raid Precautions Committee and was responsible for co-ordinating its own services with those covering fire prevention and fighting, mortuaries, emergency repairs to houses, evacuation rest centres, and emergency medical services.

The County's direct responsibilities included control of civil defence services, wardens, messengers, rescue, decontamination, mobile casualty, first aid posts (both static and mobile), public gas cleansing centres and gas identification. There were also a number of subsidiary services such as mobile canteens, salvage and stretcher parties. The Chairmen of the Emergency Committee were Lord Brooke of Oakley (September 1939 – August 1942) and Mr. Ewart Marlow (August 1942 – 46).

The County Borough had similar responsibilities, but the Chief Constable, John Williamson, acted as 'supremo' over his own force, the civil defence services and the Fire Brigade. The Committee Chairman throughout the war was Alderman A. W. Lyne.

All the above services had, in turn, to be co-ordinated with other independent bodies such as the Home Guard, St. John Ambulance Brigade and Red Cross, Salvation Army, etc.

33. Control room staff of Northampton's emergency services parade in Abington Park, November 1939.

34. A.R.P. wardens parade at Northampton, November 1939.

35. Northampton 'messengers'; messengers on foot, cycle and motor-cycle were organised to act as an alternative to telephone communications when they had been cut.

36. 'Messengers' at Blisworth.

37. An A.R.P. team, including auxiliary nurses, at Britton's farm, Birchfield Road, Northampton, 1940.

38. Head warden, wardens and messengers at Rushden.

39. Wardens give instructions on the extinguishing of incendiary bombs by use of a stirrup-pump.

40. An A.R.P. practice in Castle Street, Northampton.

41. This car-ambulance was believed to be the first of its kind in the country when converted in early December 1939. In the background is Northampton's transport depot. Another car was donated for the same purpose in January 1941 by Mr. Spencer Summers, Northampton's M.P.

42. A mobile first aid post. The County Emergency Committee had provided five of these in 1939, all converted from horse boxes. A doctor was in charge of each. There were a total of 313 static first aid posts.

43. The first county residential training school for auxiliary nurses was opened at Whilton Lodge, the home of Major and Mrs. G. R. D. Shaw. The 'crash course' lasted for two weeks. Centre front, in uniform, is Mrs. Shaw. November 1939.

44. The Duchess of Gloucester, holding bouquet, inspects ambulance workers at the First Aid Post, the 'Racecourse' Pavilion, Northampton, 14th October 1939. On her right is the Marchioness of Exeter, and between them, the Mayor, Alderman A. W. Lyne.

45. The Duchess of Gloucester accompanied by the Mayor of Northampton, Councillor A. L. Chown, visits St. Edmund's Maternity Hospital, February 1941.

46. A St. John Ambulance Brigade convalescent home in Colwyn Road, Northampton, 1942.

47. Red Cross blood transfusion team, 1945.

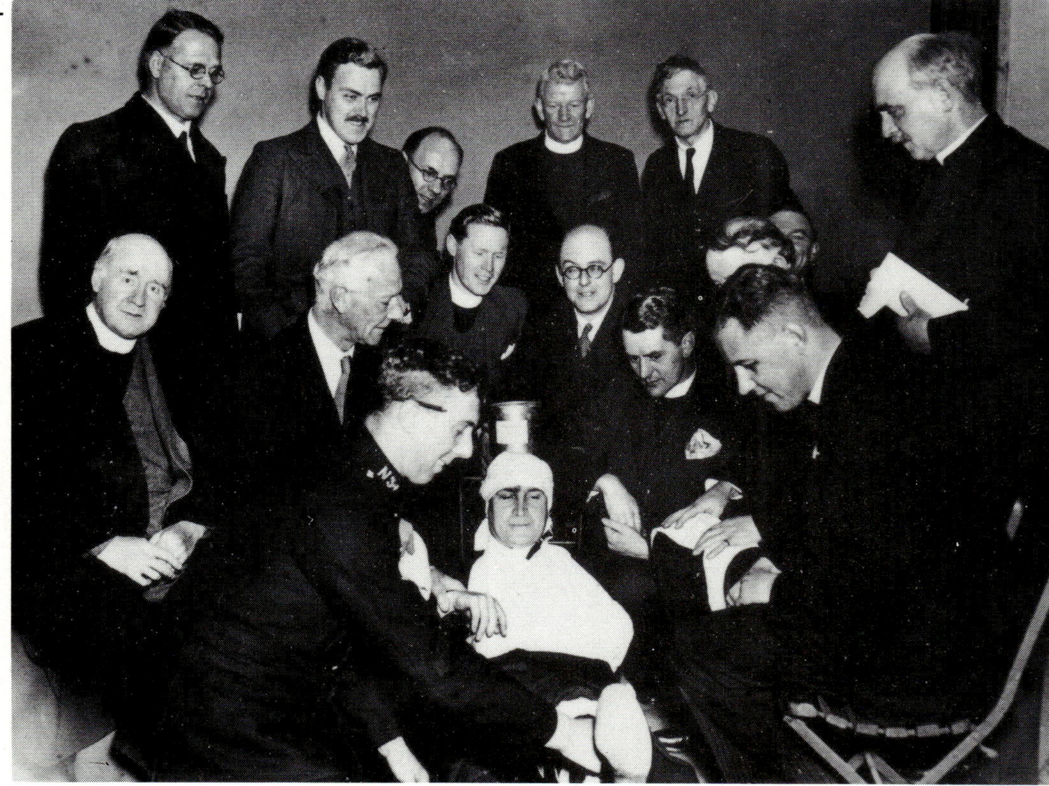

48. Northampton Free Church ministers are given instruction in first aid.

49. Civil Defence personnel followed by the Royal Observer Corps, the W.V.S. and Girl Guides parade at Duston on 24th May 1942.

50. Royal Observer Corps at Raunds, about 1943. The Royal Observer Corps, founded in the 1920s, watched the German planes after they had passed the radar chain, and so helped guide the fighters to their mark.

51. Northampton Civil Defence wardens who reinforced the County Borough of Wandsworth from 29th June to 17th September 1944.

52. The Duchess of Gloucester and Northampton's A.R.P. Controller, John Williamson, with one of the 'casualties' at an A.F.S. demonstration.

53. 'Roof spotters', members of the cast, at Northampton Repertory Theatre.

54. A section of the National Fire Service at the Mounts Station, Northampton. The N.F.S. was formed from 1,666 independent authorities in England and Wales in August 1941.
Earlier in the war (Autumn 1940), the local Auxiliary Fire Service had helped out in London's East End.

55. Pump at source of supply, River Nene, Kislingbury Bridge.

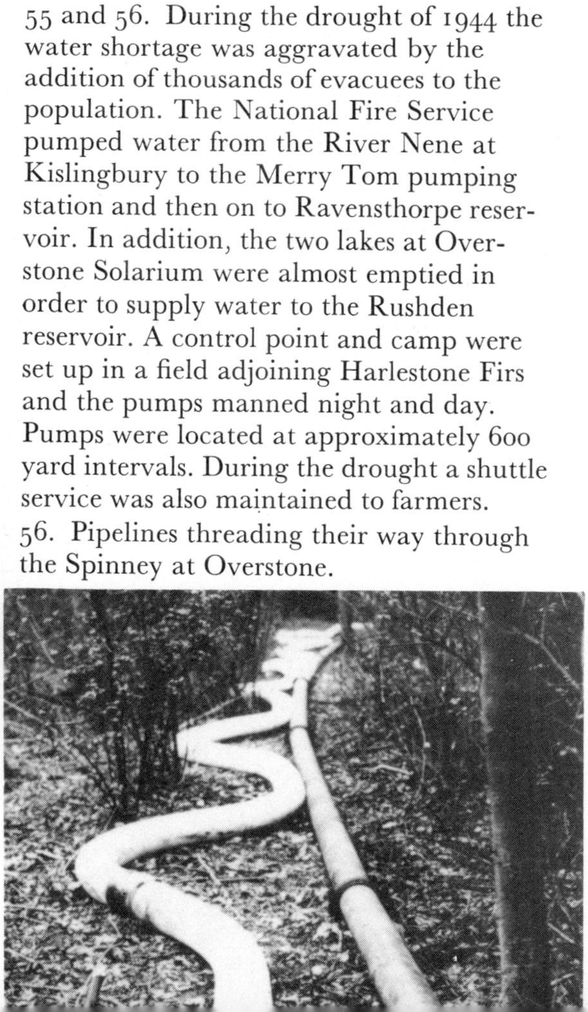

55 and 56. During the drought of 1944 the water shortage was aggravated by the addition of thousands of evacuees to the population. The National Fire Service pumped water from the River Nene at Kislingbury to the Merry Tom pumping station and then on to Ravensthorpe reservoir. In addition, the two lakes at Overstone Solarium were almost emptied in order to supply water to the Rushden reservoir. A control point and camp were set up in a field adjoining Harlestone Firs and the pumps manned night and day. Pumps were located at approximately 600 yard intervals. During the drought a shuttle service was also maintained to farmers.

56. Pipelines threading their way through the Spinney at Overstone.

57. Myra Brown 58. Winifred Parker 59. Jean Edwards

Three National Fire Service girls, all from Irchester, 1944.

60. Girls train with the National Fire Service in Northampton, January 1942.

61. Wartime Home Secretary Herbert Morrison inspects Northampton Fire Service stations in September 1942. On the right are Chief Regional Fire Officer, T. C. Patrick, and Divisional Officer, A. H. Spence.

62. The Marchioness of Northampton, August 1942. The Marchioness served as a land girl at Castle Ashby, in the W.R.N.S. and (shown above) in the Women's Auxiliary Police Corps as a driver.

63. A parade of 'special' constables in front of Northampton's Guildhall, 1942.

THE HOME GUARD

The Home Guard began life as the Local Defence Volunteers following a broadcast by Anthony Eden (then Secretary of State for War) on 14th May 1940 in which he appealed for men between the ages of seventeen and sixty five 'to come forward now and offer their services . . . You will not be paid, but you will receive a uniform and will be armed'. The government saw the new force as a method of counteracting the use of parachute troops which had proved so effective in the German sweep across Belgium and Holland. The need to watch the skies for the invader is emphasised in Brophy's handbook (64) where all the aeroplane identity silhouettes refer to troop-carrying planes. For a time the L.D.V.s were referred to as the 'para-shooters'. Brophy defines the duties of the L.D.V. as follows

1) Guarding important points
2) Observation and reporting – prompt and precise
3) Immediate attack against small, lightly armed parties of the enemy
4) The defence of roads, villages, factories and vital points in towns to block enemy movements.

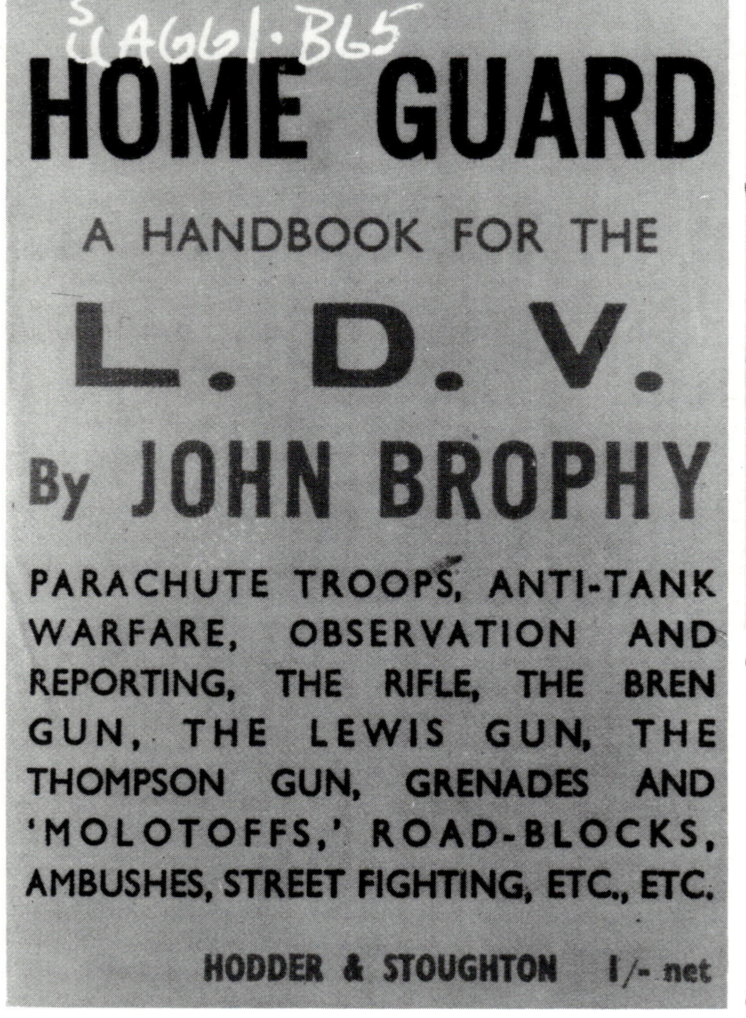

64

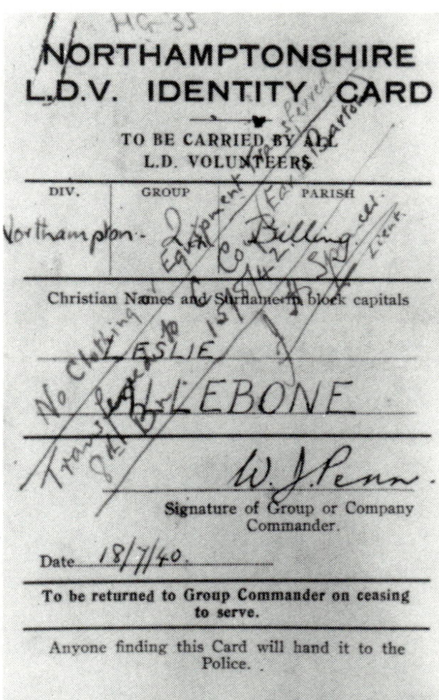

NORTHAMPTONSHIRE
L.D.V. IDENTITY CARD

TO BE CARRIED BY ALL L.D. VOLUNTEERS

DIV.	GROUP	PARISH
Northampton		Billing

Christian Names and Surname in block capitals

LESLIE
...LEBONE

W. J. Penn
Signature of Group or Company Commander.

Date 18/7/40

To be returned to Group Commander on ceasing to serve.

Anyone finding this Card will hand it to the Police.

65. L.D.V. identity card.

66. L.D.V.s of the 12th (Northampton) Battalion, E. Company. On the right is Captain R. J. Marfleet. The change of name to 'Home Guard' was first suggested by Winston Churchill in a broadcast on 14th July, and was formally announced on 23rd July. On 3rd August units were given county titles as with the regular army. Gradually the organisation became more efficient and better armed, and later in the war the Home Guard supported the army in manning anti-aircraft guns. Early in 1942 membership of the Home Guard became compulsory.

67. Home Guards check identity cards at Spinney Hill, Northampton, during 'Operation Scorch', December 1941. This was the first large scale exercise which portrayed invasion conditions. The R.A.F., Home Guard, Civil Defence and 50,000 troops took part.

68. Unarmed combat

70

71

69. The infamous pike. In October 1941 consignments of pikes were issued to the Home Guard for street fighting. A wave of ridicule swept the country as people visualised middle-aged men trying to halt a well equipped enemy with a weapon which looked and sounded medieval. Neither publicity photographs such as this nor the statement by the joint Under-Secretary of the War Office, Lord Croft, that 'a bayonet is a useful weapon. If prolonged by a stave it is a still more useful weapon . . . ' convinced the nation.

70. A positive disguise for a sniper.

71 and 72. Training at Billing Hall. The site is now occupied by Lady Winefride's Walk. During the war the Hall, the former home of the Elwes family, was used as an army transport centre, a camp for the Czech army and for anti-aircraft training.

73. Long Buckby Home Guard paraded with their band before Admiral Sir Roger Keyes at Daventry, April 1943. The band was formed in November 1940 mainly from the Long Buckby Town and Temperance Bands.

74. The Home Guard marches through Oundle, followed by the R.A.F.

10

75. A Home Guard demonstration in Abington Park, Northampton.

76. A road block and sand-bagged firing position at Spinney Hill, Northampton, August 1941. The erection and maintenance of road blocks were Home Guard duties. There were 750 concrete cylinders in Northampton alone.

77. The checking of identity cards at Kingsley, Northampton. Note the whitened mud guards and bumpers, and hooded headlights for use in the blackout.

78. Kingsthorpe Golf Club. Obstructions were placed on golf courses to prevent enemy planes landing.

77

78

'The annual cost to the country for each Home Guard was estimated in 1944 at £9 5s (£9.25). The whole Home Guard's total budget for a year was only £16,600,000, roughly equal to a single day's expenditure on the War. The Home Guard was an enormous bargain, the cheapest army of its size and fire-power that any nation ever possessed.'
Norman Longmate *The Real Dad's Army* 1974

79. Islip and Aldwincle sections of the Home Guard.

80. The Express Lift Co. Home Guard platoon. Other firms who raised their own platoons included the Northampton Electric Light Company, the Northampton Gaslight Company, Corby Works, Wellingborough Iron Company and many others.

81. An inspection in October 1941 of the 13th (Towcester) Battalion by Major General Viscount Bridgeman, Director General of the Home Guard and Territorial Army.

82. A home-made armoured car.

83. A German wireless transmitter. On the afternoon of 7th September 1940, a man was discovered lying in a ditch in a dazed state at The Elms, Denton by an employee of farmer and race-horse trainer, G. C. Beechener. He was a spy who had been dropped by parachute the previous night, and on landing had hit his head on his wireless set – it weighed twenty one pounds. He was carrying £200 in English notes, a compass, maps, food and extra clothing, as well as a loaded pistol. His forged identity card had a Birmingham address with the street number entered after the name in the continental custom. He claimed he was a wireless expert, who had been sent over against his will.

82

83

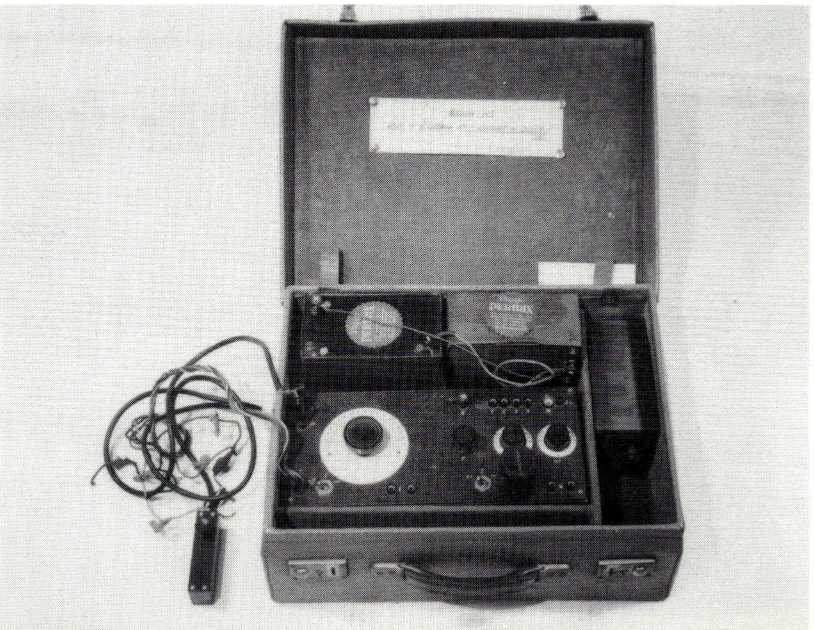

84. Band of the 12th (Northampton) Battalion Home Guard.

85. The Northover Projector in action.

86. A Spigot mortar

87. The stand down parade in Northampton Market Square, Sunday, 3rd December 1944.

88. The final march past, 3rd December 1944. The Home Guard was eventually disbanded in December 1945.

WAR DAMAGE

Although Northamptonshire was one of the areas least affected by air raids, approximately 7,800 bombs fell on the county. The bomb count consisted of 1,128 high explosives (of which only 38 fell on Northampton itself), approximately 6,500 incendiaries, a number of delayed action bombs, 14 oil bombs, 8 parachute mines, 3 flying bombs (or 'doodlebugs'), and a number of unexploded bombs. The first bombing attack in Northamptonshire took place at Kilsby, where 14 high explosive bombs fell on 16th August 1940, doing little damage. The first of 3 flying bombs fell at Creaton on 22nd July 1944. Photographs were published in the press and the location given as 'a village in Southern England' in order to confuse their German operators.

Deaths from bombing were surprisingly low, thirty five out of a total of thirty six being in the Wellingborough Police Division. 212 people were injured. In the United Kingdom as a whole by 1944 4½ out of a total of 13 million houses had been damaged by enemy action, and throughout the war over 60,000 civilians were killed.

89. 500 kilogram bomb.
On 3rd August 1942, shortly after a raid on Wellingborough (see also illustrations 101–2) Flying Officer Black, a New Zealander, flying a Spitfire, shot down a Dornier 217. Information on the Dornier's position was fed through to Flying Officer Black with the aid of a running commentary from the Royal Observer Corps. The Dornier crashed at Fox Covert Farm between Finedon and Thrapston with this bomb remaining on the bomb rack. It was excavated in September 1975 by the Kettering Aircraft Research Group (Secretary Mr. J. Holliday) and made safe by an Army Bomb Disposal Team under Captain J. Dickson.

90. The first attack on Northampton, night of 26–27th August 1940. The residents of this bungalow in Dunston were saved by their Anderson shelter. Nearby an electric cable of 4,000 volts was broken; a warden, mistaking the flashing end for an incendiary bomb, played the water from a stirrup-pump on it and was electrocuted.

91. Two land mines, the first in the county, were dropped at Pury End, Paulerspury at 9.56 p.m. on 26th September 1940. Land or parachute mines were cylinders eight feet long and two feet in diameter which parachuted down at approximately 40 m.p.h. As they did not penetrate the ground before exploding, the blast and damage were all the greater. At Pury End about fifty of the one hundred and one houses in the village were damaged, farm buildings and part of the farm-house were shattered, and eight people were slightly injured. The roof of the Dutch barn was lifted and all the rivets torn out, the roof then returning to its place. The Post Office, Wardens' Post and local pub were also damaged as were houses up to two miles away.

92. Raid on Rushden, 3rd October 1940, Alfred Street School. A Dornier bomber dropped 18 high explosive bombs, hitting Eaton's factory and Alfred Street School. A number of incendiaries were also dropped. Seven children and four adults died, and forty people were injured, eight of them seriously. The school caretaker (inset) was also injured. There was a direct hit on the school's air raid shelter but this was fortunately not in use as the public air raid warning had not been sounded. The Victoria Hotel and a number of shops and houses were also damaged.

93. Raid on Rushden, 3rd October 1940. Workmen survey damage to Eaton's boot factory.

94. Raid on Rushden, 19th November 1940. The bombs were dropped in gardens between two streets. Four adults and one child were killed and many cottage properties damaged.

95. St. Andrew's Hospital, Northampton, 15th January 1941. The central portion of the infirmary wing for a length of 183 feet was totally demolished; one end was partially demolished for 97 feet, as was the other end for 71 feet. The same stick of bombs damaged the cemetery on the other side of Billing Road.

96. Damage to Billing Flax Mills, April 1941.

Stirling bomber crash in Northampton, 15th July 1941. All members of the crew bailed out successfully except the pilot, whose body was later found in the north part of the town. The only civilian casualty was a fire-watcher who was returning home. He was blown off his bike by the blast and broke his leg.

97. Looking up Gold Street towards All Saints Church.

98. This bomb lodged in a bedroom of the Queen's Head Hotel (corner of College Street) and had to be lowered out by R.A.F. bomb experts.

99. Looking towards Gold Street from George Row; on the right is All Saints Church. This photograph was published shortly after the crash, but for security reasons the bomb in the centre was painted out.

100. The type of bomber which crashed in Gold Street. It had a wing span of 99 feet.

101. Raid on Wellingborough, Bank Holiday Monday, 3rd August 1942. At 6.10 p.m. the alert was sounded in Wellingborough and other areas in the county, and almost simultaneously a Dornier 217 flew low over the town dropping four 500 kilogram high explosive bombs. The bombs fell in the middle of a block of old buildings comprising shops and business premises on the corner of Market Square, opposite the Hind Hotel; on Mather's Foundry at the rear of Midland Road; and at the back of 'working class' housing forming Winstanley Road on the one side and Newcomen Street on the other. Four women, two men and one boy were killed, and 55 (23 women, 21 men, 5 boys and 6 girls) injured. There was extensive damage to property, 43 houses being seriously damaged, 388 slightly; other damaged properties were 10 factories, 6 places of worship, 13 hotels and public houses (only one seriously), 125 shops, 2 cinemas, 5 banks and the headquarters of the Broadcast Relay Services. Injuries would have been much heavier but for two facts; Bank Holiday crowds were attending a fair on the outskirts of the town, and a long queue had just been admitted to the nearby Regal cinema. Apart from the emergency services, valuable help was received from both British and American troops who used their own tools and transport in helping clear the debris; work continued until the following Monday, 10th August.

103. Raid on Wellingborough, 22nd August 1942. At 10.53 p.m. the alert was sounded

102. The Salvation Army to the fore following the raid of 3rd August.

in Wellingborough and one minute later a plane dropped a stick of four bombs across the centre of the town. They fell in Swanspool gardens, about thirty yards behind the Council Offices; at Dulley's Yard, in Sheep Street (shown in photograph); at the rear of the G.P.O., Midland Road; and at a warehouse at the junction of Alma Street and Park Road. An 18 year old Home Guard on duty was killed, and twenty five people were injured (14 men, 7 women, 2 boys and 2 girls). There was damage to 104 houses, a café, 45 shops, 2 cinemas, 5 factories and workshops, the G.P.O., the Council Offices and the Food Office. The H.Q. of a company of the 7th Northants Bn. No. 1 Home Guard in Dulley's Yard, used as a store for ammunition and phosphorus bombs, was damaged; a fire which

broke out there was, however, soon con- 103
trolled by the N.F.S.

AGRICULTURE

As early as 1936 it had been decided that county agricultural committees would be set up in the event of war. They were to be linked to the Ministry of Agriculture and Fisheries. Despite these early plans (even provisional lists of chairmen, secretaries etc. were drawn up), the committees were not activated until the autumn of 1939, and the opportunity to undertake detailed pre-war planning was lost. However, once the committees were established they proved extremely effective, due to their direct link with the Ministry and a county organisation based upon local knowledge and advice. Northamptonshire's War Agricultural Executive Committee appointed District Committees based upon the eight Rural Districts of Brackley, Brixworth, Daventry, Kettering, Northampton, Towcester, Wellingborough and Oundle/Thrapston, though this last was divided into two administrative sub-districts. The Executive Committee also appointed sub-committees on labour, machinery, and feeding stuffs. In addition, there were District Officers who acted as reporting officers to their sub-committees and gave advice to farmers on day to day problems. The two chairmen of the committee were J. O. Adams (September 1939 – December 1940) and H. R. Overman (December 1940 – July 1946). The Chief Executive Officer was R. George, Land Agent of the County Council, and the Secretary was R. A. Barber.

There were five main depots for the committee's agricultural machinery based at existing garages located at Northampton, Thrapston, Kettering, Daventry and Towcester; a sixth was later added at Brackley. The organisation was undertaken by Honorary Machinery Officer H. Mobbs. In June 1939 there were under one thousand tractors in the county, many of them Fordsons. By the end of the war the committee alone was responsible for an additional 200 tractors, 290 ploughs, 141 binders, 180 drills, 176 sets of disc harrows, 24 combine harvesters and over 2,000 other machines. Work was done either on behalf of farmers at a cost of so much per acre, or machinery was hired out.

104. Pre-war delays in obtaining supplies resulted in the country entering the war with negligible reserves of imported feeding-stuffs such as barley, maize and oilseeds and cakes. Steps were taken to encourage the growth of crops suitable for feeding stuffs. Here threshing of sunflower seeds is taking place on Home Farm, Little Billing.

105. Mr. Charles Mackaness looks out from a field of semi-dwarf sun flowers. Each flower held about three thousand seeds.

106. Cutting Holdfast wheat with a combine harvester, 1941. The overall width is 14 feet, the cutting bar 6 feet. The yield was 13 sacks per acre. 'Dad' is Mr. A. Waterston.

107. The wartime drive for increased agricultural output hastened the decline of horses on the land – they decreased from 12,581 to 8,865 between 1939 and 1945.

108. Regular farm workers picking peas on Home Farm, Little Billing.

109. Schoolboys help with the potato harvest at Weston Favell. During the six seasons of the war many thousands of tons were picked by Northamptonshire children under arrangements made between the County Education Committee and the War Agriculture Executive Committee.

THE WOMEN'S LAND ARMY

The Women's Land Army came into existence in June 1939, when a register was opened of women who would be prepared to give up their ordinary jobs for farm work if war came. With the outbreak of war an organisation was soon set up in Northamptonshire under the Chairmanship of Countess Spencer; the Secretary was Mrs. Elizabeth Simpson of Higham Ferrers. Courses were established at the Northamptonshire Institute of Agriculture, Moulton, and in October the Duchess of Gloucester visited the Institute, where she met forty trainee land girls from all walks of life.

Early recruits included a chauffeuse, hairdresser and factory and office workers. When they had finished their training, the girls constituted an additional labour force for farmers or took the place of workers who had been called into the armed services. They were either employed long term on individual farms, or were housed in hostels where they could be allocated to a number of farms for various jobs according to need. The Y.W.C.A. staffed and ran the hostels. The girls worked a 48 hour week, and they were expected to have left for work by 7.30 a.m. A 'hostel' often meant Nissen huts.

In 1941 the wage was 28s (£1.40) per week and rose to 48s (£2.40) in 1944. Out of this the girls had to pay their board and lodging. In Northamptonshire there were over twenty hostels, each in charge of a forewoman; every week, time sheets were taken into County Hall, Northampton, where wages for each hostel were worked out. The overall day to day management of the County Women's Land Army was the responsibility of a Labour Officer (male) assisted by two Labour Officers (female). They in turn were responsible to the Labour Sub-Committee of the County's War Agricultural Executive Committee.

110. Trainee land girls arrive at Moulton Institute of Agriculture.

111. A lecture in progress. On the left is Miss Janet Strang, Deputy Principal of the Institute.

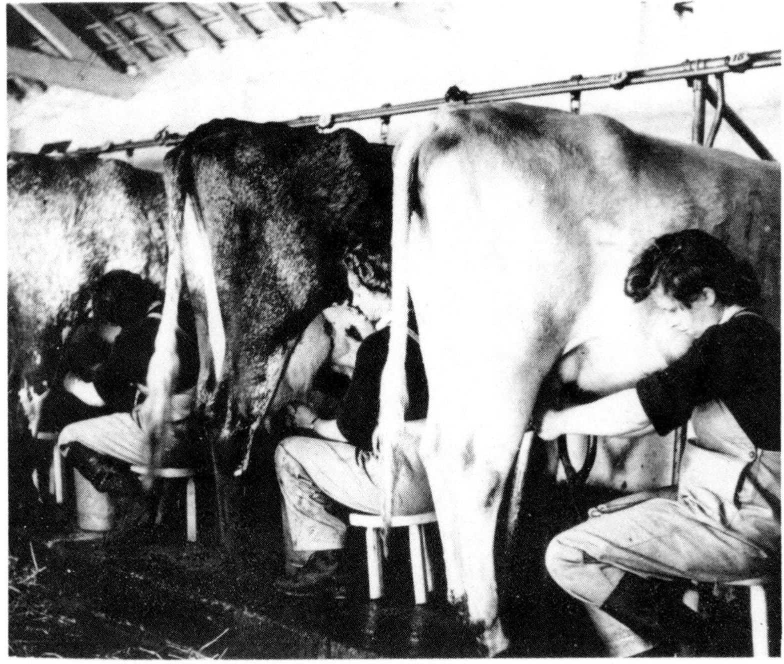

112. Milking by hand and machine. Most of the county's training in milking was done at Moulton.

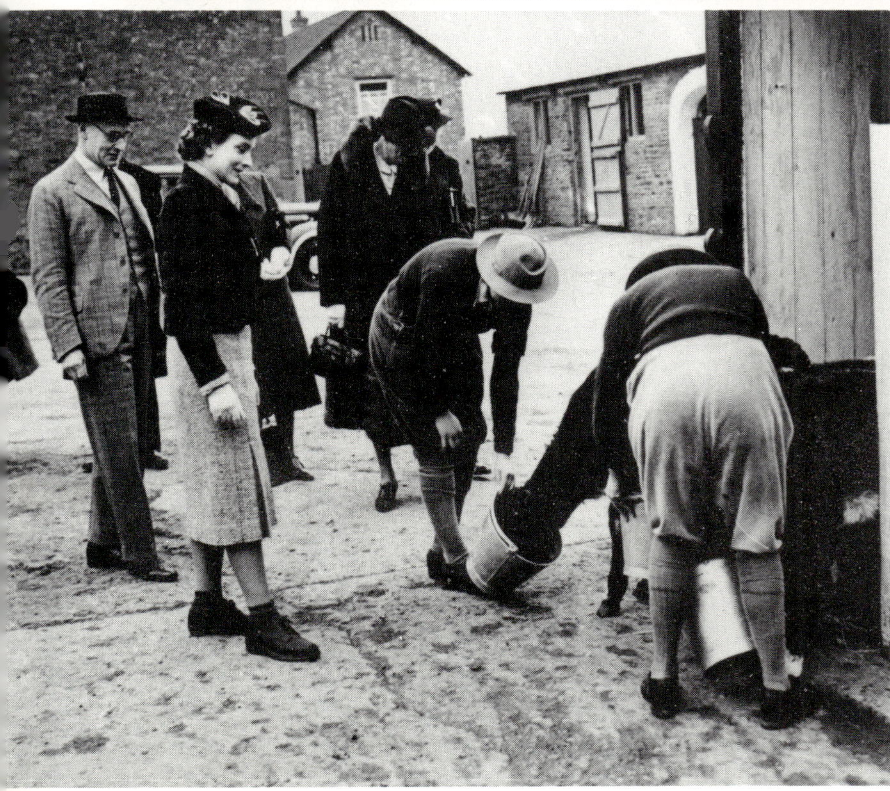

113. Feeding time for a Moulton pig. A system of rationing animal feeding stuffs was introduced 1st February 1941 with two classes of coupons for cereals and protein.

114. The Duchess of Gloucester visits Moulton on 28th March 1941. On the left is the Institute's Principal, Mr. W. A. Stewart, a well known wartime broadcaster on agriculture.

116

117

115. A recruiting display in the foyer of a Northampton cinema, April 1940. Third from left is Countess Spencer, County Chairman of the Women's Land Army; she took the keenest interest in the girls' welfare, making a monthly visit to Moulton to see each new intake of trainees. On her left is Mrs. Elizabeth Simpson, County Secretary. By October 1942, 1,500 land girls were working in the County, and at one time the figure reached almost 2,000.

116. Instruction on tractor mechanics at Moulton; the instructress (front right) is Peggy Bush (now Mrs. H. B. Parkinson) who was later appointed as one of the two female Labour Officers.

117. Girls relax with instructress Peggy Bush.

118. Work on Tom Turney's farm, Quinton.

119. Work on Home Farm, Little Billing.

120. Land girls from the Desborough hostel join in a local fête in aid of hospitals. Fourth from left, front row, is forewoman Betty Spanton (later Mrs. A. J. Linnell). Land girls throughout the country had been angered by the terms which had been laid down for their demobilisation – they could justly compare their treatment unfavourably with other services. For instance, they were not eligible for resettlement grants as were members of the Civil Defence. The girl top right labelled 'Demobbed' is symbolically wearing a shirt, the only garment which the land girl claimed she could take into 'civvy street' with her.

121. German prisoners of war photographed in Salcey Forest with Labour Officer R. Warwick of Earls Barton (second from left) after the war. German and Italian prisoners of war played an important role in the agriculture of the County, although as Tom Turney wrote in 1947, initially they were available in small numbers only as 'it took us some time to catch them'. At their height, there were 4,610 helping on farms, housed in eight parent camps, two sub-camps and seventeen hostels. Their work was controlled by 22 Labour Officers who received their training at Brixworth. P.O.W.s proved particularly useful in pioneer work on ditching and draining schemes – there were over 5,000 of them – approved by the War Agriculture Executive Committee.

	Permanent Grass	Temporary Grass	Wheat	Barley	Oats	Mixed Corn	Pulse Crops	Root Crops for Stock Feeding	Cabbage Kale etc. for Stock Feeding	Sugar Beet	Potatoes	Broken-up Grassland bearing first arable crop	Total Arable Acreage
1939	383.174	19.920	37.672	10,612	12,624	206	5.778	5,776	2,109	2,463	1,573	——	112,672
1940	356.576	19.784	38.095	19,104	27,211	2,001	2,268	6,897	3,864	2,478	1,899	32,164	140,434
1941	287.181	18,429	60,070	28,012	44,701	6,326	6,502	8,448	5,359	2,664	6,654	70.833	208,649
1942	262,996	32,930	72,665	20,457	32,882	5.292	8.776	8,068	3.998	4,382	9,819	26,056	224,849
1943	220.910	42,658	96.236	26.973	27.328	6.559	11.931	8,835	4,497	4,894	11,611	46.274	267,359
1944	194.154	62,768	95.180	31,583	29.973	3.640	13,817	8.998	4,663	5,057	12,714	31,942	292,323
1945	187,970	80,218	75.296	40,812	31.659	4.089	9.706	8,961	4.813	4.742	13.095	13.986	298.499

In 1936 the government accepted certain principles upon which a wartime food policy would be based. These were to increase as much as possible home production of foods which gave the largest and quickest yield and were bulky to import. In particular, priority was given to wheat, potatoes, oats, eggs and sugar beet, but the production of meat, milk and fresh vegetables at near pre-war levels was encouraged. The immediate effect upon counties was to increase the amount of arable land. The effectiveness with which this was accomplished is clearly shown in the statistics extracted from agricultural returns for June in 1939–45.

	Dairy Cows	Heifers in Calf	Bulls for Service	Other Cattle	Sheep	Pigs	Poultry	Horses
1939	32,900	9,498	1,821	100,334	368,865	35,826	571,526	12,581
1940	32,373	11,456	1,940	107,463	389.947	32,366	605.047	12,035
1941	32,703	9,132	1,772	92,200	292,181	21,724	494,802	12,056
1942	30,811	14.599	2.031	88,989	270,193	19.499	427,580	10,907
1943	33,764	12,183	2,195	83.279	216,184	15,759	344.242	9,943
1944	33,849	11,250	2,254	86,652	193.552	17,929	384.201	9.132
1945	32,553	13,064	2,129	94,342	205,770	24,101	456,059	8,865

INDUSTRY

The approach of war saw a massive redirection of British industry; much that had previously been aimed at civilian consumption was turned to the war effort. In 1943 the number of cars produced for civilian use was nil (280,000), motor cycles 2,000 (47,000), wireless sets 50,000 (1,900,000), pianos nil (50,000). The figures in brackets refer to production in 1935.

Many firms in Northamptonshire found themselves making a valuable contribution in the fight against Hitler.

BOOTS AND SHOES

Northamptonshire manufacturers produced a wide range of footwear during the war, including the standard marching boot, later modified with a rubber sole for tank and jungle warfare, shoes without nails for explosives factories, long boots with special ties at the top as protection against mosquitoes, nursing sisters' shoes, footwear for army firemen and motor cyclists, a variety of on and off duty shoes for American servicemen and, towards the end of the war, demobilisation shoes.

Not least important were the boots specially made for our airmen, and shown in 122 are an electrically heated boot, an R.A.F. wader,

122. R.A.F. appeal window of Rushden Boot and Shoe School, July 1943. Inset: Airman's 'escape' boot.

a W.A.A.F. shoe, the standard flying boot, and an ankle boot. Secret work was also undertaken. In 1940 airmen who bailed out over the continent had their escape jeopardised because the resistance movement could not obtain civilian shoes for them. In an effort to improve upon the expedient of airmen tying a pair of shoes to their belts when flying, A. Haynes asked his partner in Haynes and Cann Ltd., R. J. Kitchin, to design a boot which could be turned into a shoe. This Kitchin did, and the 'escape' boot went into production late in 1940; by 1941 some 80 to 100 pairs per week were being produced. The boot, made of box calf, had a knife inserted in a slit to one side of the sheepskin lining, and this could be used to cut off the leg of the boot, leaving a good quality – some said too good a quality – Oxford shoe. Hollow heels containing a compass, and a lace incorporating a flexible file, could be provided at special government request. The boot proved so effective that in 1943 the Air Ministry asked for a large increase in production, specifying that the leg should include 30 layers of shrapnel-prook silk. Due to a shortage of box calf, the leg of the boot was henceforth made of black suede (see inset above). Occasionally silk maps were included in the leg of the boot, only appearing however, when washed in water with the airman's tie. Other work included making shoes for secret agents, when a worn look was simulated by making the impression of a foot in the insole and polishing it; the seat sock would have the mark of a firm only partly printed on it, usually of a town which had been heavily bombed, so that its true origin could not be traced.

123. Aircraft instrument panels being manufactured in no. 2 factory, May 1943.

THE EXPRESS LIFT COMPANY, LTD.

The Express Lift Company, with three satellite factories at Harlestone Road, Northampton, St. John's Street Station (corner of Fetter Street, Northampton) and Syston, Leicestershire, made a wide variety of wartime products. Their main work was on aircraft instrument panels for Wellington bombers, in close liaison with the Royal Aircraft Establishment at Weybridge. Other products included shell hoists for destroyers, pusher hoists on aircraft carriers, parts for the Oerlikon gun, shells, gear units for anti-submarine protection, and bomb aimer panels and other aircraft parts.

124. The 7.2″ shell factory, May 1943.

125. A general view of the 7.2″ shell factory.

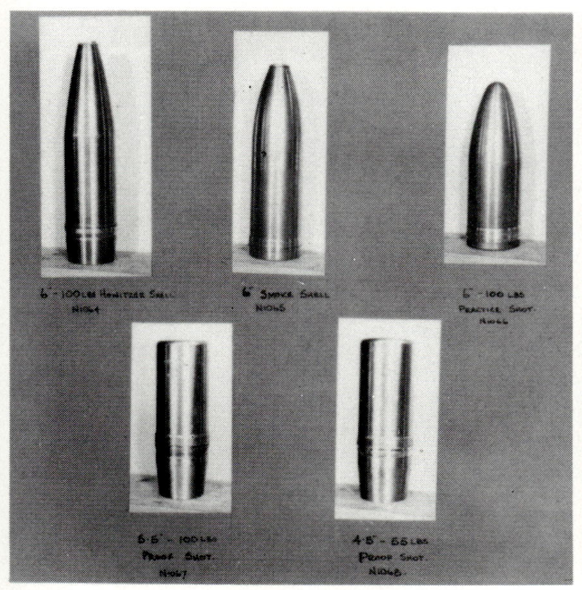

126. Sample shells.

127. A break for workers at the Air Ministry Gas Cylinder Testing Station, Wellingborough Gas Works, 1943. The gas was used for barrage balloons.

128. The Duchess of Gloucester visits Charles Wicksteed's of Kettering, manufacturers of industrial sawing machines (used especially for sawing iron bars) which were supplied to many firms and organisations including the Navy and the Ministry of Defence. December 1943.

129. Grinding One shop at British Timken, Duston, roller bearing manufacturers, traditionally based in Birmingham. The outbreak of war and heavy bombing raids on the industrial Midlands necessitated dispersal of priority industries. A site for a new Timken factory was found in Duston in 1941, and only five and a half months later, March 1942, production started. Shortly after this the Birmingham factory received several direct hits.

130

VISIT OF THE KING AND QUEEN, 4 MARCH 1943

130. Kettering Clothing Manufacturing Co-operative Society Ltd.

131. Sears Shoe Company, Northampton. The King is trying to get a nail out of his shoe which he had trodden on in the factory.

132. Northampton Gas Company.

131

132

133. A pipeline being wound onto the drum.

THE MAKING OF PLUTO (PIPELINE UNDER THE OCEAN)

Operation PLUTO consisted in laying two types of pipeline under the English Channel in order to pump petrol to the allied forces on the continent. One of these (called the *Hamel* pipeline) was manufactured by Stewarts and Lloyds of Corby, now part of the British Steel Corporation. A total of 1,000 miles of pipe was made, some 250 miles in 20 ft. lengths, the rest in 40 ft. lengths. These were flash-welded together and coiled round a large drum called a 'conundrum'. The Royal Navy then took over, the drum being towed by two tugs, whilst a third helped control and steady the drum from behind. Many *Hamel* pipelines were laid from Dungeness and the Isle of Wight. When laying was completed they were connected to the thousand mile oil pipe grid which brought the petrol from the northern ports. When fully operational, PLUTO pumped about one million gallons of petrol across the Channel daily. The scientist responsible for the techniques of making and laying *Hamel* was Dr. J. S. Blair.

134. A pipeline being laid.

BASSETT-LOWKE, LTD.

The construction of models in order to test the design and capabilities of projects was much used. Bassett-Lowke Ltd. of Northampton built proving models of three types of bridging, the Inglis bridge, the subsequently more successful Bailey bridge, and a railway bridge intended to cross bomb craters or waterways. The firm also made models of invasion tanks, vehicles, mobile guns and possibly most important, Mulberry Harbours; full size, these were concrete caissons, 200 feet long, 56 feet wide and 60 feet high, which were towed across the Channel and formed prefabricated harbours through which men and supplies flowed following the establishment of beachheads on the French coast. Other work included assessors (full size) built into the wings of fighter aircraft to assess marksmanship, and models of Stuka dive bombers with a simulated 'dive' to train anti-aircraft marksmen.

135. An early bridge design.

136. Mulberry Harbour model.

WALLIS and LINNELL, LTD.

Samples of service uniforms manufactured by Wallis and Linnell Ltd., Kettering. During the war the firm manufactured over 200,000 garments, mainly for the services, including the first W.A.A.F. uniform.

137. i) Coat and uniform made specially for 43 stone member of Bristol Home Guard, with 73″ waist.

ii) N.F.S., 1942.

iii) W.A.T.S. khaki drill, 1941.

iv) W.A.A.F., 1942.

v) W.A.A.F. khaki drill, 1941.

vi) A.T.S., 1942.

vii) Royal Observer Corps, 1942.

AIRCRAFT ASSEMBLY AND REPAIR

The following photographic record was made shortly after the end of the war

138. An aerial view of Sywell airport and hangars. In the background are camouflaged Armstrong Whitworth hangars where Lancaster bombers were assembled. Manufacture of the components was carried out at several dispersal factories, including Barratts' shoe factory, Frecknall, Barnard and Scott, and the Northampton Corporation 'tram' sheds. The components were brought to Sywell by road, assembled and then flown to Bitteswell in Leicestershire. Between July 1942 and November 1943 some 100 Mark IIs with Hercules engines were completed.
In the foreground are (left) the main assembly hangar, no. 3 site, for Wellington bomber assembly by Brooklands Aviation, Ltd., and (right) 6th Elementary Flying Training School. In the background on the right is Brooklands no. 1 site, Holcot Lane, where completed Wellington bombers were tested and flown. Not shown is no. 2 site at Boothville.

THE REPAIR OF WELLINGTON BOMBERS BY BROOKLANDS AVIATION, LTD.

Components of the aircraft were repaired at fifteen dispersal points (including United Counties Garage, Desborough; Sywell repair factory, no. 2 site, Buttocks Booth; Smith's Garage, Northampton Road, Moulton; Butcher's (operating) Corona Works, The Avenue, Spinney Hill, Northampton; Butcher's Garage, Kettering Road, Northampton; Abbott's Garage, Earls Barton; Abram's Garage, Earls Barton; Blanchflower's (operating) Victoria Street, Kettering; Blanchflower's Garage, Northampton Road, Kettering; Thompson's Garage, Tresham Street, Kettering; A. E. Smith (operating) Polwell Lane, Burton Latimer; A. E. Smith, Carrington Street, Kettering, supported by Hadden's Furniture Warehouse; and Macrae's Garage, Rockingham Road, Kettering). They were then brought together for assembly at Sywell. As each aircraft was completed it was test flown, in the early days by test pilot Alex Henshaw, who flew daily from Castle Bromwich in a Spitfire; later Brooklands had its own test pilot, based at Sywell. At the height of its activities Brooklands employed 2,700 workers. some redirected from local shoe factories.

139. No. 2 site, Buttocks Booth. The fuselages show the 'geodetic' design of the aircraft's framework, pioneered by inventor Barnes Wallis. Although this made it difficult to repair, it also gave great strength, and enabled the Wellington to sustain tremendous damage from anti-aircraft fire. In the foreground and to the left are Lancaster bomber wing tips and tail units being repaired.

140. No. 2 site, Buttocks Booth. The main fuselages are now covered.

141. In the foreground aircraft are being dismantled; at the rear other aircraft are being re-assembled.

142. The main assembly hangar no. 3 site. The inner wing and engine being fitted. In the far background an aircraft has been fitted with the outer wing (i.e. outer main plane).

B
B
B
C

143. A completed aircraft waits at no. 1 site, Holcot Lane. Writing in August 1945 the managing director J. W. Massey, said 'we have completed 1,700 aircraft during the war . . . In fact, we were, at the height of our activities the largest repairers in the country . . . Another repair centre is at Brooklands (Surrey) where . . . we have dispersal points at Sunbury-on-Thames and High Wycombe . . . We were also given an M.A.P. factory to operate at Doncaster . . . We then became sole repairers of Wellington type aircraft . . . During the period when the Wellington was used so extensively for raids over the continent, we kept working parties at all operational Stations for carrying out repairs to aircraft damaged by flak. This was a very necessary service as the R.A.F. were particularly short of skilled ground personnel . . . I was able to run all the factories with executives drawn from pre-war employees, and did not employ any additional personnel from outside sources, for the management side . . . our E.P.T. [Excess Profit Tax] standard was based on the company's "Lean years", with the result that every penny of profit earned on the repair side has been paid back in tax. In other words, we have done the job for nothing – and I am rather proud of the fact!'

LIFE AT HOME

144. Northampton Guildhall, February 1940.
The winter of 1939-40 was the coldest for forty-five years.

GERMAN "PEACE"

This jackboot tramples on the lives of men, of women and of children in all the countries over which the Nazis rule to-day.

A German " peace " does not just mean a change of government. It would mean that everybody's daily life, whether poor or rich, would be run the Nazi way—everybody slaves to German masters ! Their spies everywhere. Their guns and rubber truncheons bossing people, from morning until night. Those who do not please them imprisoned, tortured or shot.

Remember what has happened wherever Germans rule.

A German girl—she might have been your daughter—was sent to prison for 18 months for dancing with a Polish prisoner. A shopkeeper got 6 years' imprisonment for selling cloth without a ration card. A whole family got 5½ years' imprisonment for listening to a non-German wireless station. Forty-six people were executed for " black-out " offences. These were Germans. In Poland, 150 Boy Scouts, between 10 and 16 years of age, were shot down by machine-guns in the market square. They might have been your sons.

The Gestapo Rules

When the Germans enter a country, their terrible secret police come into every home. There is a knock at the door. They have come to seize your house. This happened one night to 6,000 people living in a town in Czecho-Slovakia. They were turned out, into the winter street, to make room for Germans. The same thing happened to people on farms in the country : the farms were taken : the owners left to starve.

Or the secret police have come because somebody in the house is accused of having said something, some time, against the Germans. It may be that he belongs to a Trade Union. That is a crime for which thousands have died. Anyhow, he is taken away. His family never see him again. They never know why or where he is gone. At last, one day, a small parcel is delivered. The wife or mother opens it. Inside are ashes : all that is left of her dear one. This is not imaginary—it actually happened.

The Fate of the Children

Fathers and mothers have to see their children taught, by Nazi teachers, to spy on their parents ; and watch them being hammered into a Nazi shape They have to see them going short of food. Rations for non-Germans are smaller than for Germans. The little savings they have pinched and struggled to collect, for their children's future, are seized. Home life is broken up : the breadwinner is compelled to go to work wherever his German master sends him. He has to leave his family behind, and is paid so little that he cannot help them. Czech and Polish, Danish and Dutch workers have been sent away to toil in Germany.

It shall not be

Make no mistake—a German " peace " would mean ruin and misery for all of us—poor and rich, worker and employer, young and old.

But there shall be no German " peace."

We have a great Army; an Air Force incomparable in quality and courage: a Navy more powerful than any combination against it. We have behind us the resources of the Empire and of the United States. Our own workers are piling up supplies by their magnificent devotion. This is the People's war against German "peace."

THE BRITISH PEOPLE WILL WIN

Issued by the Ministry of Information

145. Anti-Nazi propaganda; a leaflet issued in 1940.

146. Mr. Ewart Marlow leads the march during Citizen Sunday, 2nd June 1940, at Desborough. He became Chairman of the County's Emergency Committee in 1942.

147. Ration book staff at work in the Guildhall, Northampton, October 1939.

FOOD RATIONING

148. Ration book 1941 (original size $5\frac{1}{2}'' \times 4\frac{3}{8}''$). Initially there was no food rationing, but as food supplies were reduced to allow ships to bring in more armaments, official rationing was introduced in gradual stages from 8th January 1940. Each person had allocations of essential foods (butter, sugar etc.) whilst in December 1941 a certain number of additional points were allocated to each ration book holder, and these points could be spent as required on a wider range of foods (e.g. tinned goods, dried fruit, breakfast cereals, rice, biscuits).

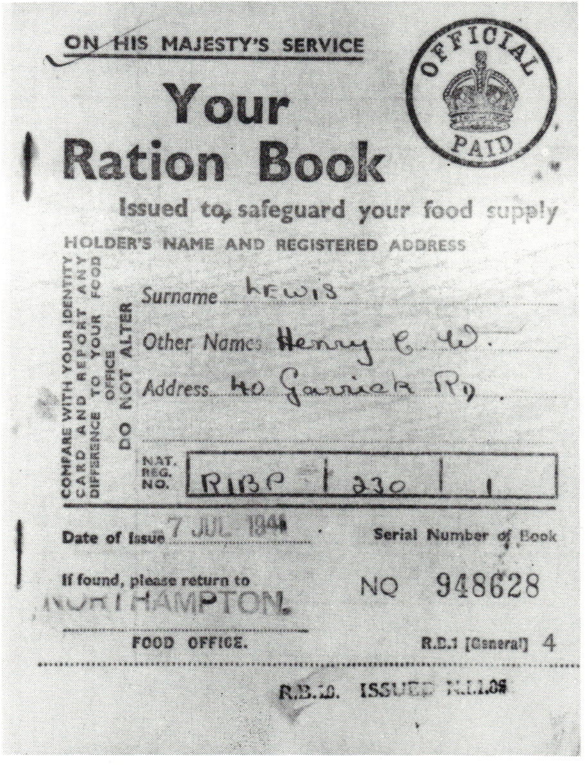

ON HIS MAJESTY'S SERVICE

OFFICIAL PAID

Your Ration Book

Issued to safeguard your food supply

HOLDER'S NAME AND REGISTERED ADDRESS

COMPARE WITH YOUR IDENTITY CARD AND REPORT ANY DIFFERENCE TO YOUR FOOD OFFICE

DO NOT ALTER

Surname LEWIS

Other Names Henry C. W.

Address 40 Garrick Rd.

NAT. REG. NO. RIBP | 230 | 1

Date of Issue 7 JUL 1941

Serial Number of Book

If found, please return to

NORTHAMPTON.

FOOD OFFICE.

NQ 948628

R.B.1 [General] 4

R.B.10. ISSUED

149. A queue for tomatoes (an unrationed commodity) on the Market Square, Northampton.

150. A queue for eggs in Northampton's covered market, 1941. By 1943 approximately 35% of all eggs eaten were 'dried' eggs and the average consumer obtained only 30 shell eggs during the year.

151. A confectioner's window display during rationing. Rationing of sweets and chocolate was introduced in July 1942.

152. Troops help with the 'Dig for Victory' campaign on the Spencer Estate, Northampton, 1940. At the rear with trilby hat and umbrella is Mr. W. R. Kew, Northampton Town Clerk.

A WARTIME WEDDING RECEPTION

153. A wedding took place on 8th August 1942, at All Saints Church, Northampton, between Miss Grace Elson, a well known local soprano, and Leading Aircraftsman Harry Slater. On the groom's right is best man Mr. Jack Gill of Willenhall, Staffs. The menu consisted of cold chicken, some ham and tongue, white bread (not national wheatmeal loaf) and a small quantity of butter. The main drink was fruit juice, and there was some chocolate Swiss roll.

154. The cake was iced with chocolate as the use of white icing-sugar had been made illegal from 5th August 1940.

155. The couple leave for their honeymoon, the groom now in 'mufti'. After the war he became headmaster of a school in Staffordshire.

156. Queue for coupon-free clothing in Mercers Row. The clothing shop is 'Lyons'.

CLOTHES RATIONING

157. Clothing book (actual size $5\frac{1}{4}'' \times 3\frac{5}{8}''$). Clothes rationing was introduced in June 1941. By 1943 a man could expect to buy only one pair of boots, shoes or slippers every thirteen months, a housewife one pair every eight months. Women could buy five or six pairs of stockings a year.

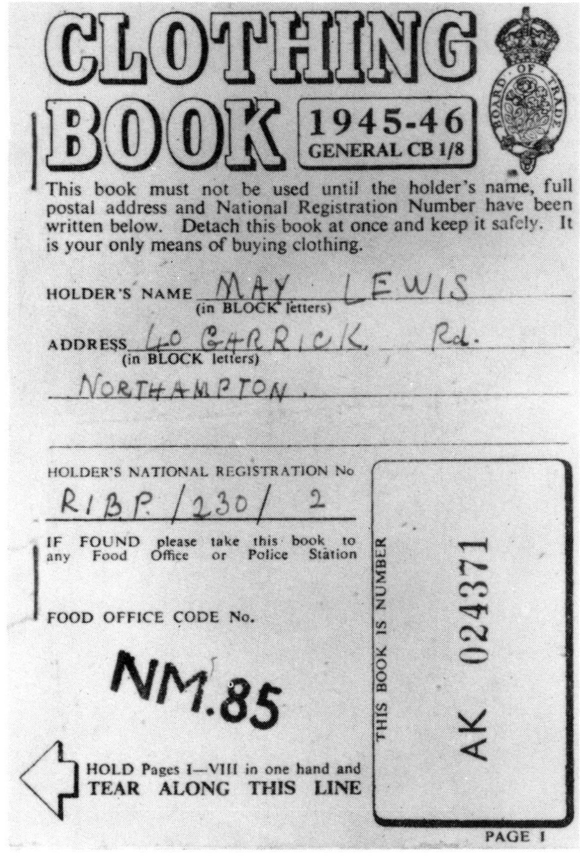

CLOTHING BOOK 1945-46 GENERAL CB 1/8

BOARD OF TRADE

This book must not be used until the holder's name, full postal address and National Registration Number have been written below. Detach this book at once and keep it safely. It is your only means of buying clothing.

HOLDER'S NAME (in BLOCK letters) MAY LEWIS

ADDRESS (in BLOCK letters) 40 GARRICK Rd.
NORTHAMPTON.

HOLDER'S NATIONAL REGISTRATION No RIBP/230/ 2

IF FOUND please take this book to any Food Office or Police Station

FOOD OFFICE CODE No.

NM.85

THIS BOOK IS NUMBER AK 024371

HOLD Pages I—VIII in one hand and TEAR ALONG THIS LINE

PAGE I

158. The well known utility mark, introduced in 1941, guaranteed a minimum quality.

A. UNITED KINGDOM. — Introduction of Clothing Rationing. - Details of Scheme.

A scheme of clothing rationing prepared in secret to ensure fair distribution of the present restricted supplies with immediate effect was announced by Capt. Oliver Lyttelton, President of the Board of Trade, in a broadcast on June 1. Buying clothing, cloth for dressmaking and other purposes, footwear or knitting-wool, will not be permissible without surrendering clothing coupons, of which each person will receive 66 for 12 months. Coupons, which will be interchangeable between husbands, wives and children, but not otherwise, may be expended anywhere in accordance with the point values shown below.

Men and Boys	Adult	Child
Unlined mackintosh, cape	9	7
Other mackintoshes, raincoats, overcoats	16	11
Coat, jacket, blazer and like ..	13	8
Waistcoat, pull-over, cardigan, jersey..	5	3
Trousers, (other than fustian or corduroy), breeches, kilt	8	6
Fustian or corduroy trousers ..	5	5
Shorts	5	3
Overalls, dungarees and like ..	6	4
Dressing-gowns, bathing-gowns ..	8	6
Night-shirt, pair of pyjamas ..	8	6
Shirt or combinations—woollen ..	8	6
Do., other material	5	4
Other undergarments, athletic vest, bathing costume, child's blouse ..	4	2
Pair of socks or stockings, bathing trunks	3	1
Collar, tie, pair of cuffs	1	1
Two handkerchiefs, knee-caps, ankle supports	1	1
Scarf, pair of gloves or mittens ..	2	2
Pair of slippers, goloshes	4	2
Pair of boots, shoes	7	3
Pair of leggings, gaiters, spats ..	3	2

Women and Girls	Adult	Child
Unlined mackintosh, cape	9	7
Other raincoats, coats (over 28 in. in length), and like	14	11
Jacket, blazer, short coat	11	8
Dress, gown, frock, and like—if woollen	11	8
Do.—other material	7	5
Gym. tunic, girl's skirt with bodice..	8	6
Blouse, sports shirt, jumper, bed-jacket	5	3
Skirt, divided skirt	7	5
Slacks	8	8
Shorts	5	3
Furs, ties, and like	5	5
Overalls, dungarees, and like ..	6	4
Apron, pinafore	3	2
Dressing-gown, bathing gown ..	8	6
Pyjamas	8	6
Nightdress	6	5
Petticoat, slip, combinations, camiknickers	4	3
Other undergarments	3	2
Pair of stockings	2	1
Pair of socks (ankle length) ..	1	1
Collar, tie, pair of cuffs	1	1
Two handkerchiefs..	1	1
Scarf, pair of gloves, mittens, muff ..	2	2
Pair of goloshes	4	2
Pair of slippers, boots, shoes (including overshoes)	5	3
Pair of leggings, gaiters	3	2

CLOTH PER YARD.

Width	Wool*	Other Cloth Except Jute
Not over 3 in.	Exempt	Exempt
3 in.— 9 in.	½	⅓
9 in.—15 in.	1	⅔
15 in.—21 in.	1½	1
21 in.—27 in.	2	1⅓
27 in.—33 in.	2½	1⅔
33 in.—39 in.	3	2
39 in.—45 in.	3½	2⅓
45 in.—51 in.	4	2⅔
51 in.—57 in.	4½	3

* Cloth containing more than 15 per cent of wool.
Hand Knitting Wool, 1 coupon for 2 oz.

Retailers will cut the required coupons from customers' cards and pass them on to wholesalers in exchange for fresh supplies (with special rules for shopping by post).

Exemptions from rationing: (*a*) persons who have lost all their clothing through enemy action will receive an extra year's supply of coupons to replenish their wardrobe, and in the case of partial loss a corresponding proportion; (*b*) persons receiving money

159. Details of clothes rationing at the time it was announced, June 1941, taken from Keesing's Contemporary Archives, May 31 – June 7, 1941.

160 and 161. Two of over 60 such cartoons produced by Fougasse (Kenneth Bird) during the war.

162. Street furniture was painted with white lines to prevent accidents in the blackout, when all house windows had to be covered, and the only street lighting allowed was the shaded beam of a hand torch and heavily hooded car head-lights.

163. Ammunition was stored on the road-sides in many parts of the country, in this case near Great Billing.

163

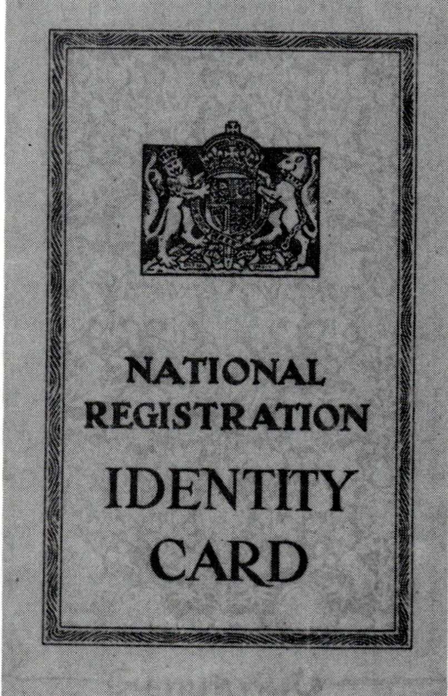
NATIONAL
REGISTRATION
IDENTITY
CARD

164. On 29th September 1939 a National Registration census recording particulars of every citizen was compiled, followed by the issue of an Identity Card, containing name, address and National Registration number.

SALVAGE

165. Railings opposite St. Giles' Church, Northampton, being taken away for scrap.

166. The scene at West Bridge Depot, Northampton.

167. Jim Campion with a street organ borrowed from the local council, collecting scrap metal for the war effort in Raunds, 1941.

NOTICE
TO RAILWAY PASSENGERS

NOTICE IS HEREBY GIVEN

that, due to the National Emergency, the following alterations in Passenger Train travel, as applying to the Railways in Great Britain, will come into force on and from MONDAY, 11th SEPTEMBER, 1939:-

1. **Passenger Train Services.**
   The Passenger Train Services will be considerably curtailed and decelerated. For details see the Company's Notices.
2. **Cancellation of Reduced Fare Facilities.**
   Excursion and Reduced Fare facilities (except Monthly Return, Week-end, and Workmen's tickets) will be discontinued until further notice.
3. **Season and Traders' Tickets.**
   Season and Traders' tickets will continue to be issued.
4. **Reservation of Seats, Compartments, Etc.**
   The reservation of seats and compartments, and saloons for private parties will be discontinued.
5. **Restaurant Cars and Sleeping Cars.**
   Restaurant Car facilities will be withdrawn, and only a very limited number of Sleeping Cars will be available.

By Order

11th September, 1939. THE RAILWAY EXECUTIVE COMMITTEE.

168

169

170

THE RAILWAYS

168-70. Services were cut by 30% with the result that trains were infrequent, crowded and, apparently, unheated. Every effort was made by the government to reduce unnecessary journeys to the minimum with such posters as 169 above. The effect on non-essential freight was similar, as the scene in Northampton's Castle Station, 170, shows.

171. Miss Hilda Mallard of St. James, Northampton, Northampton's first woman railway guard. As early as 1941 women had taken jobs as railway porters and horse van drivers.

172. A conductress in August 1940.

173. Women learn the 'mechanics' of driving. They helped in ferrying wounded soldiers from hospitals to convalescent homes and met soldiers off trains at a time when transport and fuel were short.

174. Packing parcels for prisoners of war are (left to right) Miss Dorothy Gage, Lady Hawley, Miss Diana Deterding and Lady Irene Haig. Northampton, January 1941.

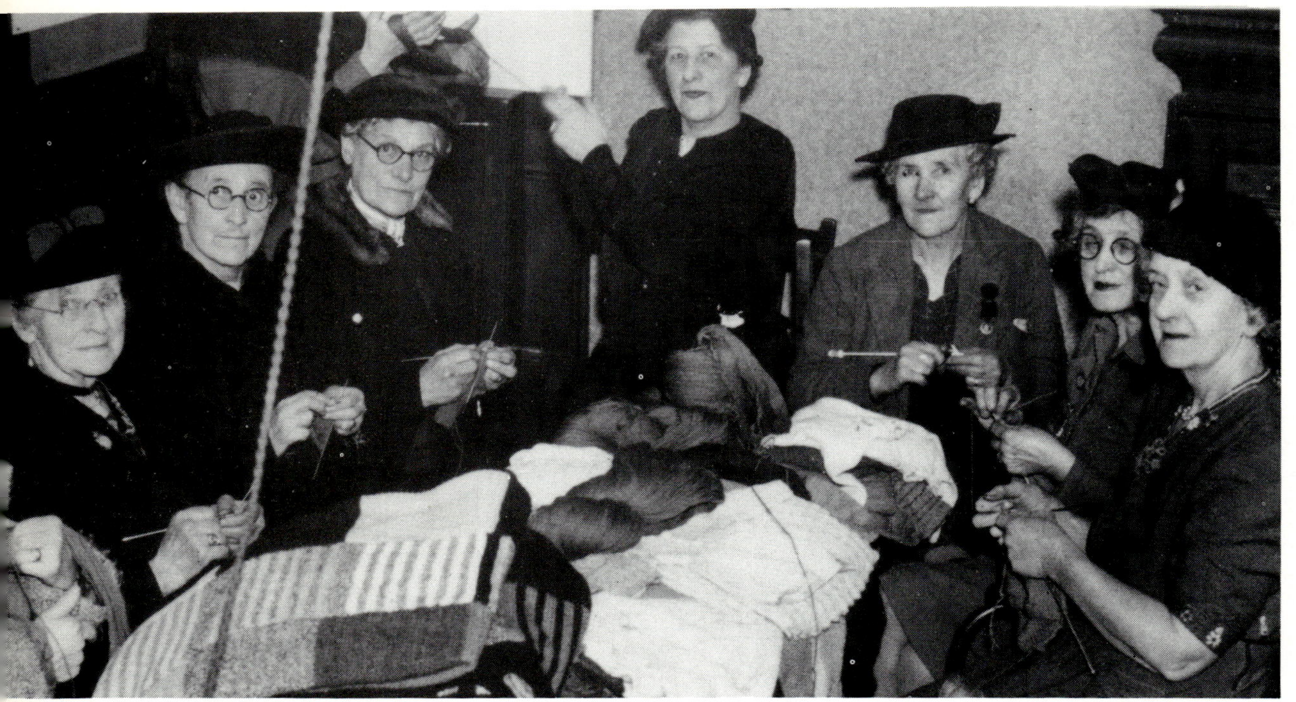

175. Knitting circles produced 1,500 garments each week for the Merchant Navy's Comfort Fund.

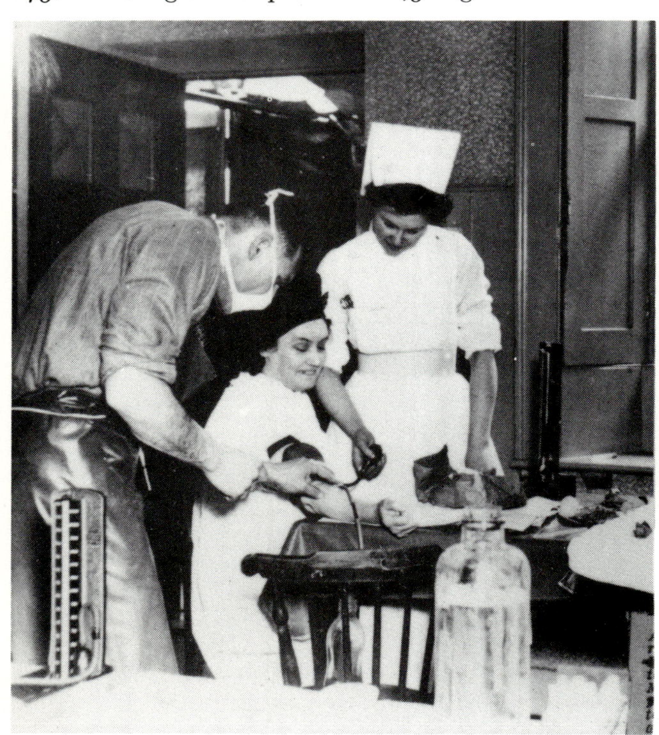

176. Dr. G. S. Sturtridge, Medical Superintendent of Northampton General Hospital, taking a blood transfusion from one of 30 volunteers at Paulerspury, 2nd March 1941.

177. Unusual transport to a Women's Institute group meeting. The W.I., at the request of the government, had mammoth jam making sessions, the jam being sold through the shops on ration. In 1941 Northamptonshire had 140 jam making centres. W.I.s also sold produce through market stalls and helped with salvage drives.

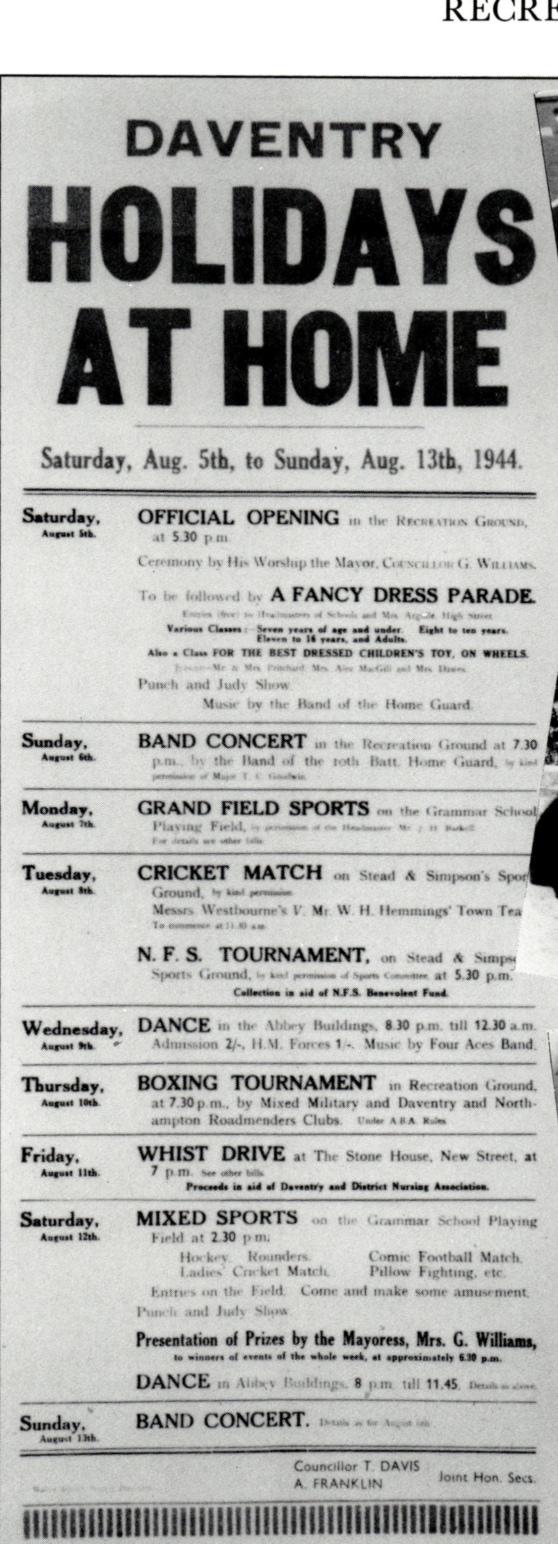

DAVENTRY

HOLIDAYS AT HOME

Saturday, Aug. 5th, to Sunday, Aug. 13th, 1944.

Saturday, August 5th.
OFFICIAL OPENING in the RECREATION GROUND, at 5.30 p.m.
Ceremony by His Worship the Mayor, COUNCILLOR G. WILLIAMS.
To be followed by **A FANCY DRESS PARADE.**
Various Classes:—Seven years of age and under. Eight to ten years. Eleven to 16 years, and Adults.
Also a Class FOR THE BEST DRESSED CHILDREN'S TOY, ON WHEELS.
Judges—Mr. & Mrs. Pritchard, Mrs. Alec MacGill and Mrs. Dawes.
Punch and Judy Show.
Music by the Band of the Home Guard.

Sunday, August 6th.
BAND CONCERT in the Recreation Ground at 7.30 p.m., by the Band of the 10th Batt. Home Guard, by kind permission of Major T. C. Goodwin.

Monday, August 7th.
GRAND FIELD SPORTS on the Grammar School Playing Field,
For details see other bills.

Tuesday, August 8th.
CRICKET MATCH on Stead & Simpson's Spor Ground, by kind permission.
Messrs. Westbourne's V. Mr. W. H. Hemmings' Town Tea
To commence at 11.30 a.m.

N. F. S. TOURNAMENT, on Stead & Simps Sports Ground, by kind permission of Sports Committee at 5.30 p.m.
Collection in aid of N.F.S. Benevolent Fund.

Wednesday, August 9th.
DANCE in the Abbey Buildings, 8.30 p.m. till 12.30 a.m. Admission 2/-, H.M. Forces 1/-. Music by Four Aces Band.

Thursday, August 10th.
BOXING TOURNAMENT in Recreation Ground, at 7.30 p.m., by Mixed Military and Daventry and Northampton Roadmenders Clubs. Under A.B.A. Rules.

Friday, August 11th.
WHIST DRIVE at The Stone House, New Street, at 7 p.m. See other bills.
Proceeds in aid of Daventry and District Nursing Association.

Saturday, August 12th.
MIXED SPORTS on the Grammar School Playing Field at 2.30 p.m.
Hockey. Rounders. Comic Football Match.
Ladies' Cricket Match. Pillow Fighting, etc.
Entries on the Field. Come and make some amusement.
Punch and Judy Show.
Presentation of Prizes by the Mayoress, Mrs. G. Williams,
to winners of events of the whole week, at approximately 6.30 p.m.
DANCE in Abbey Buildings, 8 p.m. till 11.45. Details as above.

Sunday, August 13th.
BAND CONCERT. Details as for August 6th.

Councillor T. DAVIS
A. FRANKLIN
Joint Hon. Secs.

178. Holidays at home.

179. A day out and picnic at Billing Aquadrome. 180. Mother and children in Abington Park, Northampton. 181. A group of sailors back on leave relax at the Plough Hotel, Northampton, December 1939.

182. Skating at Wicksteed Park.

185

183. Audience at symphony concert at Brooklands Aviation, Ltd., Sywell.

184. Theatre bill, 6th April, 1942.

185. The Beverley Sisters were evacuated to Northampton; twins Teddie and Babs worked at the *Chronicle and Echo*.

186

187

186. Popular coloured singer Adelaide Hall at the New Theatre, Northampton.
187. Tommy Handley of ITMA fame entertained in Northampton and Kettering during the war: here he is in the Plough Hotel, Northampton.
188. Home Guard Tattoo.

189. Will Hay's fellow comedians Moore Marriott and Graham Moffatt. They came to Northamptonshire during the war; Moffatt became licensee of a public house in Braybrooke and Marriott lived for several years in Everdon, where he founded a social club.

7th BATTALION NORTHANTS

HOME GUARD

TATTOO

Dog and Duck Ground, Wellingborough

WHIT MONDAY, MAY 25th, 1942

Commencing 3.0 p.m. :-: Dancing 8 - 10.30.

ADMISSION - ONE SHILLING

JUVENILES HALF PRICE

P.T.O.

188

189

190. The mobile theatre of 'The Keynotes', Northampton's concert party, with a group of V.I.P.s at the handing over ceremony. The entertainers were escorted at night to army camps, gun emplacements, etc. without knowing their destination.

191. War Weapons Week in Northampton, 23rd-30th November 1940. Such events were organised to encourage people to buy National Savings, War Bonds etc.

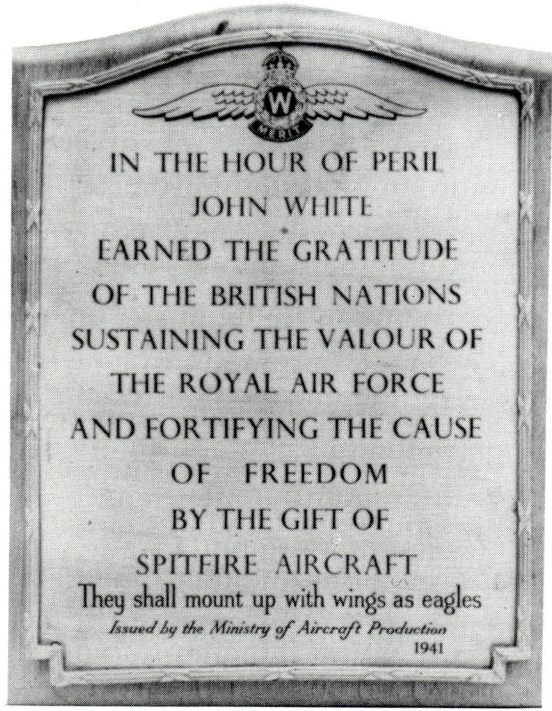

192. Plaques such as this were issued in order to encourage fund raising for the war effort.

193. Mrs. Stokes of Lowick, publicising the National Savings campaign.

194. On the bridge of mock destoyer *H.M.S. Payupansmile* is First Lord of the Admiralty, A. V. Alexander.

WARSHIP WEEK IN NORTHAMPTON,
25 OCTOBER – 1 NOVEMBER 1941

195. The Navy parades to support Warship Week.

196. Miss Britannia and her retinue at the Warship Week ceremony.

197. A captured German plane on view at Wellingborough during War Weapons Week, 25th Jan.-1st Feb. 1941.

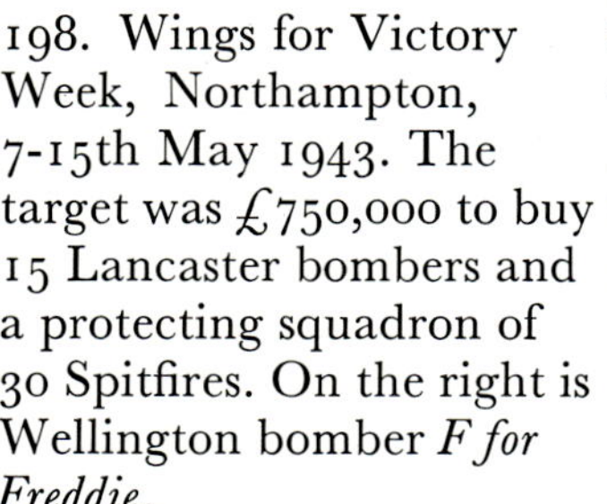

198. Wings for Victory Week, Northampton, 7-15th May 1943. The target was £750,000 to buy 15 Lancaster bombers and a protecting squadron of 30 Spitfires. On the right is Wellington bomber *F for Freddie*.

199. The Duke and Duchess of Gloucester with Prince William, photographed at their home, Barnwell Manor, summer 1943. The Prince was born in December 1941. The Duke was the third son of King George V. He was Colonel in Chief of a number of regiments during the war. He served throughout the Battle of Flanders and became Chief Liaison Officer to G.H.Q. Home Forces in August 1940. After the war he became the first royal Governor General of Australia. He died in June 1974.
The Duchess, now Princess Alice, Duchess of Gloucester, was daughter of the 7th Duke of Buccleuch of Boughton House. Her many wartime responsibilities included that of Colonel in Chief of the Northamptonshire Regiment, and Air Chief Commandant W.A.A.F. Throughout the war she was involved in an almost continuous round of official visits to hospitals, factories, army units and a multitude of other organisations.

200. United States airmen from Polebrook and Molesworth airfields, and servicemen from the wartime hospital at Lilford Hall were free to use the grounds and swimming pool at Barnwell Manor. Here service men play and apparently sing at the old castle, on an unidentified occasion.

A FAMILY AT WAR

201. Evacuee Audrey Batley of Ipswich, with Mr. and Mrs. Lewis and their daughter Georgina.

THE LEWIS FAMILY OF NORTHAMPTON

Many Northamptonshire families contributed to the war effort in various ways. Mr. H. C. W. Lewis of 40 Garrick Road, Northampton, kept a detailed record of the involvement of his family. Both he and his elder son, Ernest, were employed in Northampton's shoe industry.

202

202. Fifth from left is Georgina Lewis, a member of the St. John Ambulance Mobile Voluntary Aid Detachment, who is being seen off from Northampton's Castle Station in February 1942. She went first to Aldershot, where she nursed both allied and German casualties at Cambridge Military Hospital. She later served in the Royal Free Hospital and the General Lying-in Hospital, finally joining the Princess Mary Royal Air Force Nursing Service. After the war she married an R.A.F. pilot.
Others in the photograph from left to right are, Mr. Lewis, Georgina's father; Ernest Lewis, the elder son who appeared on the photograph by accident – he had just arrived on another platform; aunt Mrs. G. Staughton, a St. John Ambulance nurse stationed at the first aid post at Northampton's 'Racecourse' Pavilion; Alderman Burrows, Mayor of Northampton in 1934; Pte. R. Akers and Mrs. Lewis.

204. At the end of his embarkation leave, August 1942, prior to the invasion of North Africa, Ernest is seen off by (left to right) Mrs. M. Beckley, her husband Pte. C. Beckley of the Northamptonshire Regiment, Mr. Eric Warner who later kept Yardley Gobion Post Office, Mrs. Lewis, Mr. Richard Garratt and Mr. Lewis.

204

203. Philip Lewis, younger son, is seen here (fourth from left, centre row) as a member of the Warwickshire Home Guard platoon which guarded Hillmorton Radio Station. Later in the war he served in the Royal Engineers. Extreme left, front row, is Trevor Philpot, later to become a well known B.B.C. television reporter.

CAS/N'HANTS/1618
(If replying, please quote above No.)

Army Form B. 104—83

Record Office.

19

SIR ~~OR MADAM,~~

I regret to have to inform you that a report has been received from the War Office to the effect that (No.) 5885881 (Rank) PRIVATE

(Name) LEWIS Ernest Henry

(Regiment) The Northamptonshire Regiment

was ~~posted as~~ reported "missing" on the 17th November, 1942 in North Africa.

The report that he is missing does not necessarily mean that he has been killed, as he may be a prisoner of war or temporarily separated from his regiment.

Official reports that men are prisoners of war take some time to reach this country, and if he has been captured by the enemy it is probable that unofficial news will reach you first. In that case I am to ask you to forward any postcard or letter received at once to this Office, and it will be returned to you as soon as possible.

Should any further official information be received it will be at once communicated to you.

I am,

SIR ~~OR MADAM,~~

Your obedient Servant,

Colonel

Officer in charge of Records.

IMPORTANT.

Any change of your address should be immediately notified to this Office.

Wt. 30051/1249 400,000 (16) 9/39 KJL/8812 Gp 698/3 Forms/B.

206. This card was the first communication giving the prisoner of war camp Ernest was held in.

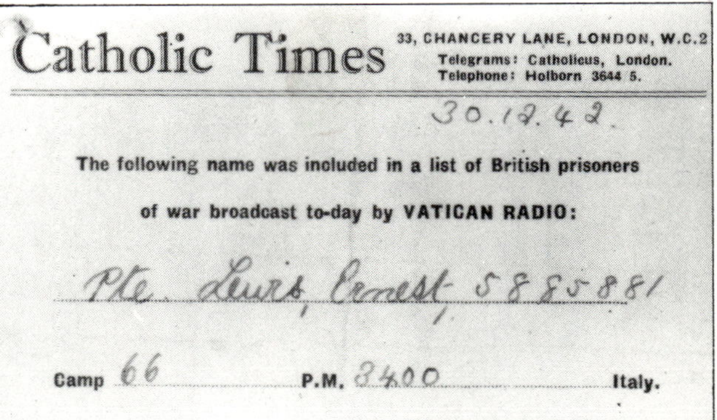

Catholic Times

33, CHANCERY LANE, LONDON, W.C.2
Telegrams: Catholicus, London.
Telephone: Holborn 3644 5.

30.12.42.

The following name was included in a list of British prisoners of war broadcast to-day by VATICAN RADIO:

Pte. Lewis, Ernest, 5885881

Camp 66 P.M. 3400 Italy.

207

My dear, Mother (post mark date)
(*Data del timbro postale*)

I am alright (I have not been wounded ████████
Sto bene (non sono stato ferito) (o) sono
████████). I am a prisoner of the Italians
stato ferito leggermente). Sono stato catturato dagli Italiani
and I am being treated well.
e mi trovo bene.

Shortly I shall be transferred to a prisoner's camp and
Nei prossimi giorni sarò trasferito in un campo di
I will let you have my new address.
prigionieri del quale vi comunicherò l'indirizzo.

Only then I will be able to receive letters from you
Soltanto allora potrò ricevere la vostra corrispondenza
and to reply.
e rispondervi.

With love ERNEST (signature)
Saluti affettuosi (firma)

207. The date on the back of this pre-printed message is 11th March 1943. Later Ernest was moved to a German P.O.W. camp, Stalag IV G at Oschatz.

205. This notification was received on 17th December 1942. It was followed on 22nd December by the news that Ernest had been taken prisoner.

208. The first photograph from the P.O.W. camp.

210. Family and relatives are reunited, Christmas 1945.

209. Ernest is released and returns home, May 1945. With him are Mr. and Mrs. Lewis, Ernest's uncle, Mr. George Lewis, his son Roy and wife Nancy. At the front, Micky and Rex.

SNAPSHOTS FROM HOME

211. The scheme relied upon volunteer photographers who were willing to visit families in their home surroundings and send photographs to the servicemen. The cost was borne by the volunteers, who were given priority by retailers in the purchase of film which was then scarce. The photographs shown here are chosen from the 101 families covered by Mr. H. C. W. Lewis of Northampton. One of his photographs was used in a national advertisement for the scheme.

Y.M.C.A.

Send a snapshot from home!

THE "SNAPSHOTS FROM HOME" LEAGUE.
4, Great Russell Street, London, W.C.1.

212. Mrs. A. C. Watts and children, Wellingborough Road, Northampton. Mr. Watts was in the 73rd Regiment, Royal Artillery. He served in Algeria, took part in the invasion of Sicily and Italy and, after arrival at Naples, was transferred to a security office in Austria. He was demobilised in 1946.

213. Mrs. A. C. Whiting and children, Euston Road, Northampton. Mr. Whiting started the war in the Royal Norfolks but was then transferred to the R.A.O.C. He was sent abroad at the end of 1940 and served in Egypt, Greece, the western desert and in the invasions of Sicily and Italy. He was demobilised in October 1945.

214. Mrs. H. J. Mann and children, Kenmuir Avenue, Northampton. Mr. Mann served in the Royal Artillery in Iraq, Egypt and Libya. After withdrawing to Mersa Matruh his column was ambushed and he was captured. He was first taken to Naples, then transferred to a German Stalag, ending in a camp in Czechoslovakia. Many prisoners worked in local industries which were bombed by both British and American planes. He was released in May 1945 weighing under 8 stone compared with a normal 11st. 4 lbs.

THE ARMY

215. National Service booklets arrive at Northampton G.P.O. for house-to-house distribution, January 1939.

216. Northamptonshire Regiment reservists 'answer the call' at Northampton Barracks, September 1939.

217. Canadian troops arrive at East Park Parade, Northampton, Summer 1940.

218. American troops march down Gold Street, Kettering. A film is being made for showing in the United States.

219. A map reading class at the R.A.O.C. officers' training school, Rushton Hall, winter 1940-41

220. Manoeuvres in the snow for officers training at Rushton Hall, January 1941.

221. A.T.S. girls help with food preparation at Northampton Barracks, September 1939.

222. 'Ready for any emergency' ran the caption to this photograph in the *Northampton Independent* August 1939. The A.T.S. had just completed camp training, and are shown here at the Northampton Depot. The difference between the new recruits – privates in the second and third rows – and the N.C.O.s and officers, is noticeable. Centre front is Mrs. R. M. Raynsford, Company Commander.

223. The Marquess of Exeter, Lord Lieutenant of Northamptonshire, inspects an A.T.S. contingent on Northampton's Market Square, 25th January 1940.

224. A.T.S. 'Red caps' (military police) at their billet in St. Giles' Street, Northampton.

225. Sgt. Haslam and C.S.M. Walkinshaw offer refreshments to three United States airmen who baled out of their plane over Brixworth, 23rd December 1943.

226. Girls of a War Office special demonstration platoon rest on their way between Brackley and Northampton.

CASTLE ASHBY

227. The NAAFI canteen and recreation huts on the north lawn. The house was requisitioned for military purposes during the war.

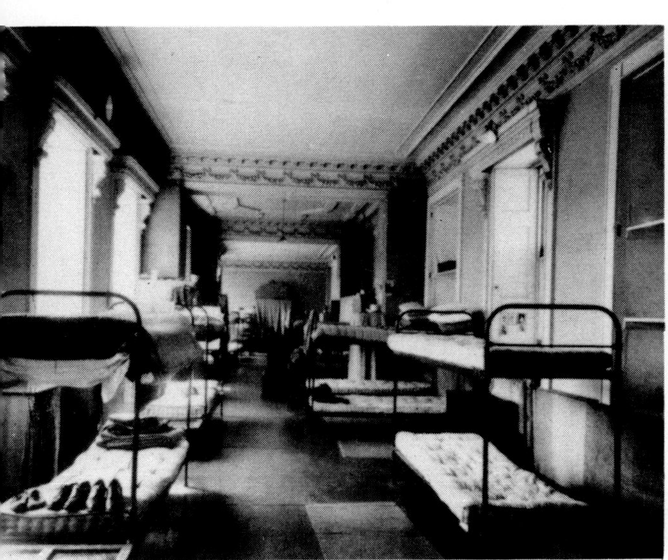

228. The Long Gallery, Castle Ashby, which slept forty-three A.T.S. girls. The Marquis of Northampton and his family lived in the south-west corner of the house, whilst male military personnel slept in the stables and specially built Nissen huts.

229. The Avenue, Castle Ashby. During preparations for the invasion of Normandy over six thousand vehicles were parked in the Avenue.

230. Troops at Castle Ashby, about 1941.

DAVENTRY A.A. BATTERY, LOCATED NEAR THE TRANSMITTING STATION

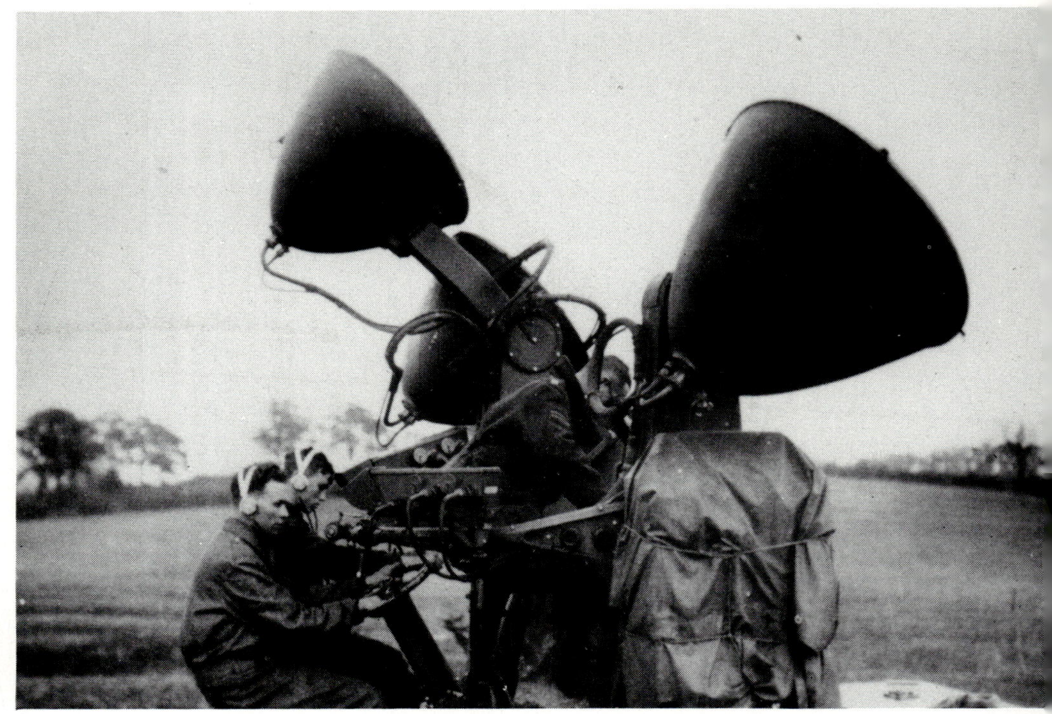

231. An early form of listening device.

232. Estimating the height of aircraft.

233. A searchlight.

234. Loading the anti-aircraft gun.

THE NORTHAMPTONSHIRE REGIMENT

The Northamptonshire Regiment consisted of six battalions. The 1st was the regular battalion of the regiment serving overseas prior to the war. They had been in India since 1928. After a period on internal security, the 1st left for the Burma front in December 1943, and fought in that campaign until April 1945. The 2nd was the home based regular battalion before the war. It saw service at Dunkirk, Madagascar, North Africa, Sicily, Italy and north west Europe. The 4th was raised in 1939 as a territorial battalion. It saw service in north west Europe in 1945 and was disbanded in 1946. The 5th was a pre-war territorial battalion, and served, as did the 2nd, at Dunkirk, North Africa, Sicily and Italy. The 6th, raised in 1940, was used solely for coast defence and draft finding; it was disbanded in 1946. The shortlived 70th (young soldiers) Battalion was raised in 1940 and disbanded in 1943. It was employed on training and airfield defence. During the war the Northamptonshire Regiment lost 54 officers and 889 other ranks.

235. The 4th Battalion, Northamptonshire Regiment, being inspected by Lt. General Sir Harry Knox at Latimer House, Chalfont, April 1940. On his left is Lt. General Sir John Brown. On the extreme left is Lt. Colonel J. Lingham. The battalion was raised by Colonel J. G. Lowther in April 1939, when the government decided to double the strength of the Territorial Army.

236. Colonel D. E. Taunton, O.C. 1st Battalion, uses his radio during the Burma campaign.

237. The North African campaign. Men of the 5th Battalion, Northamptonshire Regiment, march through Tunis after fierce fighting.

238. Infantry assault troops of the 2nd Battalion, Northamptonshire Regiment, wait on the quayside at Catania prior to the invasion of Italy.

239. The Italian campaign. Clearing up Argenta, 18th April 1945, the aftermath of a battle in which the 5th Battalion forced their way into the town supported by tanks and flame throwers.

THE NORTHAMPTONSHIRE YEOMANRY

The origin of the Northamptonshire Yeomanry goes back to 1794 when it was formed to help safeguard the country against possible invasion; the 2nd Earl Spencer was appointed Commanding Officer. In modern times the Yeomanry was reformed in 1921 under Major J. G. Lowther, armoured cars taking the place of horses. The 2nd Northamptonshire Yeomanry was not formed until April 1939, when the government decided to double the strength of the Territorial Army. Both 1st and 2nd Regiments, with the 1st Royal Gloucestershire Hussars, formed the 20th Armoured Corps in 1939; in 1943 the 20th Armoured Corps was itself split up, the 1st Regiment going to the 33rd Independent Armoured Brigade, the 2nd to the 11th Armoured Division. Both Regiments took part in the Normandy invasion in June 1944. The 1st Regiment fought in many battles of the Normany bridgehead, in the siege and capture of Le Havre, and the hard fighting in Holland to open up the River Maas (Meuse) and Antwerp. In January 1945 after a spell of fighting in the Ardennes 'Battle of the Bulge', the Yeomen's tanks were replaced with Buffalo amphibious troop carriers, and at the Rhine crossing in March they ferried infantry troops across for five days.

The 2nd Regiment took part in the Battle for Caen and the breakout from the allied bridgehead; it suffered heavy losses in battles over the River Orne. After further casualties in August the Regiment was disbanded, the remaining force being split up between the 7th Armoured Division, the 8th Hussars and the 1st Northamptonshire Yeomanry.

The 1st Regiment lost 6 officers and 69 other ranks, the 2nd Regiment 14 officers and 73 other ranks.

240. Valentine and Crusader tanks and crews of the 2nd Northamptonshire Yeomanry drawn up during the C. in C.'s inspection, November 1942.

241. Men of the 1st Northamptonshire Yeomanry prepare for the attack south of Caen, August 1944.

242. Cromwell tank commanders consult their maps before passing through Vassy, August 1944.

243. The C. in C. Field Marshal Montgomery crosses the Maas (Meuse) as rehearsal for the Rhine crossing, March 1945.

244. Men of the 1st Northamptonshire Yeomanry set off across the Rhine in a Buffalo, 25th March 1945.

THE AIR FORCES

Preparations for a possible war started in Northamptonshire as early as 1935, when pilot training schools were set up at Peterborough, Sywell, and Wittering; in 1938 the school at Wittering was replaced by three fighter squadrons under 12 Group Fighter Command.

During the early days of the war in 1940 most of the county's airfields were concerned with training, those at Sywell and Denton dealing with elementary training, whilst Hinton-in-the-Hedges and Croughton trained bomber crews. There were operational fighter units based at Wittering and Collyweston. R.A.F. heavy bomber units started operating from Polebrook in 1941, and experimented with the use of American B-17s – the famous Flying Fortresses, so called from the large amount of armament they carried. Initial results, using the technique of bombing from very high (30,000 ft.) altitudes, were disappointing, and included one of the unsuccessful attacks on the Gneisenau and her sister ships at Brest. Apart from inaccurate bombing results, the crews suffered from decompression effects and the cold, the engines lost power, and guns and other equipment froze up. The lessons learnt from these early experiments proved useful later in the war.

Airfield construction increased from this date until there were seventeen in the county. December 1941 saw the entrance of the United States into the war, and a total of seven airfields were eventually used by the United States Army Air Forces; four American Heavy Bomber Groups flew from Northamptonshire out of a total of forty in East Anglia as a whole.

During 1943 the B-17s concentrated on daylight raids whilst flying at high altitude in close formation, in the belief that the heavily armed aircraft would be able to defend themselves against enemy fighters. Bombers, however well-armed, proved no match for smaller, faster aircraft once an initial break in the tight formation had been made (normally by frontal attack), and in one raid thirteen out of fifteen B-17s taking part from Chelveston were lost. On 17th August, 36 out of 230 aircraft taking part were lost in a raid on Schweinfurt, the centre of the German ball bearing industry. The salvation of the daylight offensive was to be the long range escort fighter.

The bombing of Europe was not solely dependent on the Flying Fortress bases – the famous 'one thousand bomber' raids drew upon aircraft from Chipping Warden and Croughton. Nor was bombing the only function carried out – leaflets were dropped over France and Germany by planes from a number of airfields.

245. Instructors of 6th Elementary Flying Training School, at Sywell, winter 1939-40. Over 2,500 allied airmen were trained here during the war, including French and Belgian pilots. In addition many R.A.F. pilots were trained, 573 later receiving decorations or awards.
The chief instructor throughout was Wing Commander I. W. C. Mackenzie, M.B.E., A.F.C.

WITTERING

246. Hurricanes of No. 1 Squadron and Spitfires of 266 Squadron flying from Wittering, 1940.

247. Hurricane Mark 1 of No. 1 Squadron at Wittering, October 1940.

248. Aircrew of 151 Squadron, Wittering, about 1942.

249. Wittering was bombed on several occasions. This photograph was taken shortly after the Officers' Mess had been hit, 14th March 1941.

250. The Rhodesian High Commissioner Mr. S. Lanigan O'Keeffe, C.M.C., talks to Group Captain Basil Embry during a visit to 266 Squadron, Wittering, 13th May 1941. Embry became a legendary figure in the R.A.F. In 1940 he had been shot down over France whilst flying his Blenheim from Wattisham in an attack on German troops advancing on Dunkirk. After an adventurous two months he escaped through Spain. Later he became A.O.C. of No. 2 Group in the rank of Air Vice-Marshal, and developed the techniques of pin-point bombing attacks; he flew on many missions himself, masquerading as 'Wing Commander Smith' in case he fell into the hands of the enemy, who had put a price on his head. He ended his career as Air Chief Marshal Sir Basil Embry; among his awards were the D.S.O. and three bars and the D.F.C.

251. A Defiant of 151 Squadron at Wittering, about 1942. With its hydraulic high-speed turret, the Defiant could swivel its guns to bring immediate and heavy fire-power to bear upon enemy aircraft. Its success was shortlived, however, as German fighters soon discovered that it was vulnerable from almost any angle except the traditional attack from above and behind; its manoeuvrability was also poor.

252. A turbinlite Havoc of 1453 Flight, Wittering. In the nose is a searchlight for use in night fighting. The method was overtaken by advances in airborne radar.

253. R.A.F. night fighter crews prepare to board their Blenheims at Wittering, October 1940.

254. Crew of a Mitchell bomber. Rear left is Sgt. Navigator R. A. Ludgate, stationed at Chipping Warden on Wellington bombers from August to December, 1944. In November he took part in the dropping of 'Window' (thin strips of metal dropped prior to a raid to confuse enemy radar) over the Belgian coast. He was later stationed at Melsbroek, Brussels, and flew sorties to Burgsteinfurt, Dülmen, Coesfeld, Bremen, and Hamburg and took part in an attack supporting airborne troops at the crossing of the Rhine, 24th March 1945. The rest of the crew shown with him are the Canadian gunner, pilot R. Wales, and B. Barnet. Mr. Ludgate still lives in Chipping Warden.

255. Heinkel 111, 1426 Flight, Collyweston. Captured German aircraft were painstakingly reconstructed by the R.A.F. and based at Collyweston as 1426 Flight. They toured other airfields to familiarise airmen with enemy aircraft.

256. The official handover ceremony at Grafton Underwood, 5th July 1943. The R.A.F. Officer officiating was Squadron Leader C. E. B. Cooper; on the left is the station band of Wittering.

GRAFTON UNDERWOOD

Initial construction of the airfield commenced in 1940 when it was decided that it would serve as a satellite field for nearby Polebrook for use by R.A.F. Bomber Command. Two avenues of trees at nearby Boughton House were felled to accommodate it. After the entrance of the United States into the war in December 1941, Grafton was one of the first airfields to be put at the disposal of the U.S. Eighth Army Air Force. The first planes to use the airfield were twin engined Douglas Bostons of 15th Bomb Squadron. They were soon replaced by the 97th Heavy Bombardment Group operating Boeing B-17Es; later Groups 96, 305 and 384 were all to operate from there. The 97th launched the first attack on Europe by a Heavy Bombardment Group of the Eighth U.S.A.A.F. when it attacked the railway marshalling yards at Rouen Sotteville in occupied France, 17 August 1942, all aircraft returning safely. It was not until 5th July 1943 that the airfield was officially handed over to the U.S.A.A.F., when it became station 106. Grafton aircraft *Swamp Angel* was the lead aircraft of the planes which dropped the last Eighth Air Force bombs on wartime Europe, at the Skoda Works, Pilsen, Czechoslovakia, 25th April 1945.

257

258

257. Medics of 384th Group at Grafton Underwood, 1945. 384th Group flew from Grafton from late spring 1943 until the capitulation of Germany; the Group flew 316 bombing missions, and dropped 22,415 tons of bombs. Losses were heavy – 156 planes on mission alone.

258. Take off scene, Grafton Underwood, late Summer 1943.

259. An American band entertains at Grafton Underwood.

259

260. *Merrie Hell* of Grafton Underwood. An aircraft of the 546th Bombardment Squadron, she was one of five Grafton aircraft lost (out of a total of 25 lost), on a raid on Gelsenkirchen, 12th August 1943. She was hit by flak at 29,000 ft, and the nose was blown off almost to the back of the top turret; she immediately went down in flames. First Lieutenant E. J. Sierens and seven of his crew were killed, only the radio operator and rear gunner surviving.

261. Aircrew at Deenethorpe. Middle front with scarf is Boudinot Stimson, nephew of Henry L. Stimson, the United States Secretary of War, 1940-45.

262. U.S. airmen at Deenethorpe. On the left is Captain D. W. Fesmire who was to fly more than 200 missions over the South Pacific, Europe and Korea.

263. British artist Captain Bruce Bairnsfather became an official war artist with the U.S. Army in the second World War. Here he is painting his original creation 'Old Bill' on the fuselarge of a B-17 at Chelveston early in 1943. On 15th May 1943, it was irreparably damaged by fighters over Heligoland and had to be scrapped.

264. Deenethorpe air base. B-17s await maintenance, 12th January 1945. Deenethorpe was one of the later American bases to come into use in October 1943. The 401st Group lost 94 planes on 255 missions and about 40 others were either abandoned on the continent or lost over this country or on base.

Shortly after 8.30 a.m. on Sunday 5th December 1943, a B-17 with a bomb load of 6000 lbs crashed on the village of Deenethorpe. The crew of the plane ran through the village warning everyone to run to the fields before the bombs went off. The villagers lay flat in nearby ditches, and at 9.04 a.m. there was a terrific explosion which damaged every house in the village. Assistance was given by Colonel Scott of Deenethorpe airfield and Captain Sedlacek of the Czech Army Headquarters at Deene Hall. Only one villager refused to heed the warning – Charlie Adams, who was over seventy and lived alone; he was unhurt. The Cardigan Arms, although it had its roof damaged, and an attic ceiling demolished, was still able to serve drinks to sightseers.

265. American airmen at Deenethorpe entertain 800 children from Weldon, Deene, Deenethorpe, Corby and Benefield, December 1944.

266. American airmen enjoy English pub life at the Sondes Arms, Rockingham.

267. Hollywood film star Clark Gable was stationed at Polebrook. He flew five missions over Europe, and visited other American airfields during his tour of duty.

268. Marlene Dietrich sang to over two thousand U.S. airmen when she visited Deenethorpe.

269. Anthony Eden, Secretary of State for Foreign Affairs, visits Chelveston.

270. General Doolittle, the Duchess of Kent, Lady Herbert and the Group C.O., Colonel Lawrence, view Chelveston air base from the control tower, April 1945. General Doolittle commanded both Fifteenth and Eighth Air Forces during 1944-45

271. The King and Queen, with Princess Elizabeth, chat to the ground crew of B-17 *Ole Miss Destry* during a visit to Chelveston, 6th July 1944.

272. The royal party returns to the official car.

273. *Spotted Cow* to American airmen and *Spotted Dick* to Grafton Underwood villagers, this plane could be used as a 'target tug' or to help planes get into formation speedily after take-off.

274. Aircraft from Grafton Underwood in formation.

275. B-17s from Deenethorpe en-route.

276. Deenthorpe Flying Fortresses unload their bombs over the target.

277. *Silver Dollar* from Grafton Underwood goes down over Berlin with the loss of all the crew. The tail unit has just been swept away by a bomb from another aircraft above.

A RAID ON HAMBURG, JUNE 1944

The summer of 1944 was the high point of the B-17s' success. Not only had Germany's fighter force been weakened, it was consistently overwhelmed by the long-range fighter escorts which protected bombing missions. On 21st June, a one thousand bomber raid on Berlin and Basdorf was supported by 1,200 fighters. These conditions are reflected in the extract dated the previous day from the log of Technical Sgt. John Pratt, radio operator/gunner, who flew most of his missions on B-17 *Miss Fitt.* Mr. Pratt is now a newspaper reporter in the United States.

'*June 20, 1944*
Take off 0525B [from Grafton Underwood] – left England north of the Wash. Went over the North Sea to Denmark. Hit the coast midway between Cuxhaven and Flensburg. Went across Denmark and came down over the Bay of Lubeck and turned south into Germany. Bombed an oil refinery on Elbe River between Harburg and Hamburg. Dropped 12,500 lb general purpose bombs from 25,000 ft.

Flak light over Denmark. We were 4th C.B.W.[1] over the target. As we turned on I.P.[2] I could see all the other C.B.W.s going in. 1300 planes hit the Hamburg area today – it was terrific! Flak over target was the worst I've ever seen. I don't know how we got through it with only 2 holes. Only thing that saved us was Steve's[3] evasive action. I watched bombs go down and hit. Blew the refinery to hell. I saw flame & explosions go as high as 8000 ft. Smoke came up to about 20,000 ft. Target completely smashed. I looked back at target area after we turned off, and saw the 2 targets we hit in Hamburg covered with smoke and explosions. Above was the heaviest flak barrage I ever saw. You could walk on it! Also saw a number of rockets in the area.

Just before the I.P. we saw 4 ME.410s[4] go through the formation with a P-51[5] on their tails. They didn't shoot at our group, and we were too much afraid of hitting the P-51 to shoot at them.

Had a huge escort of P-38s[6] today. Came in so close I waved at one pilot from waist. Saw on[e] B-17 from another group go down in flames & explode – no chutes. Flak got him. Our group lost no planes, but lead pilot was killed & 3 crew members wounded. Several others wounded also. *Miss Fitt* O.K.[7]

Left Germany at Cuxhaven and came home by same route we went out. Could see Hamburg burning from 50 miles out at sea. Destruction terrible today. After bombs away, Steve left formation & we went out alone to avoid flak – group followed us – whole formation broke up. Landed OK at 1222B – 7 hrs – 4 hrs oxygen . . .'

1. C.B.W. Combat Bombardment Wing.
2. I.P. Initial Point; point at which bombers turned onto their target run.
3. Steve Raymond Stevens, the pilot.
4. ME.410 Messerschmitt fighter.
5. P-51 Mustang fighter.
6. P-38 Lightning fighter.
7. John Pratt was not a member of the crew on 16th July 1944 when *Miss Fitt* was shot down over Munich.

278. A D-Day beach bombed a few minutes before troops landed.

279. An aircraft with D-Day markings – these were used so that all Allied aircraft were easily identifiable.

280. Dakotas and Hadrians of the 315th Troop Carrier Group lined up at Spanhoe airfield, early March 1945. Shortly afterwards they took part in the crossing of the Rhine.

281. Relaxation for airmen and civilians at Kings Cliffe's open day, 1st August 1945.

AIRFIELDS IN NORTHAMPTONSHIRE, 1939-45

282. Only the main function of each airfield is given. The number and approximate formation of airfield runways are shown diagramatically.

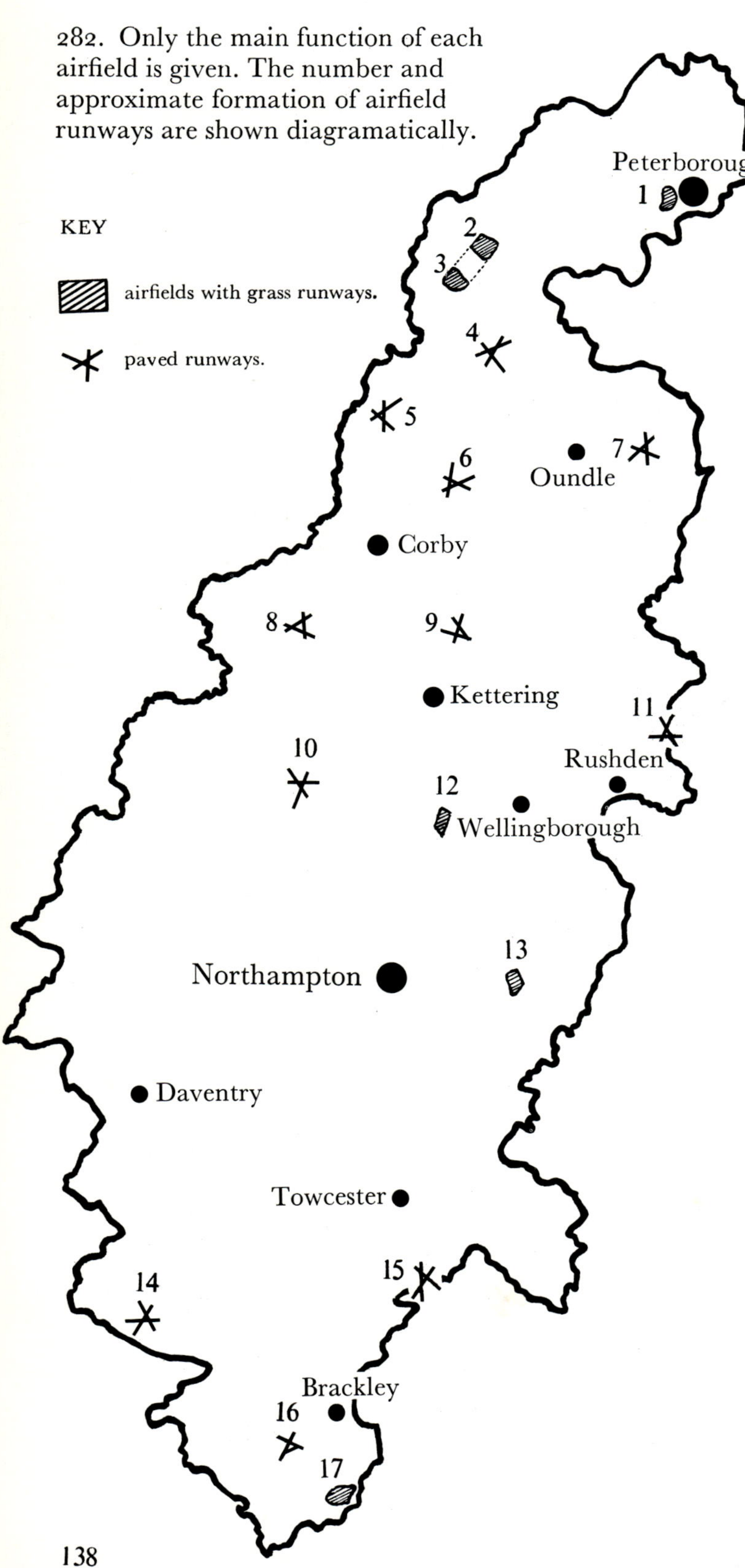

1. PETERBOROUGH.
   RAF pilot training 1939-45
2. WITTERING.
   Operational day and night fighters 1939-43
   Experimental units 1943-45
   Master diversion field 1943-45
3. COLLYWESTON.
   Operational fighter squadrons 1940-43
   Enemy aircraft flight 1943-45
   (airfield merged with Wittering 1942)
4. KINGS CLIFFE.
   RAF fighter squadrons 1941-43
   USAAF fighter groups 1943-45
5. SPANHOE.
   USAAF transport and glider group 1944-45
6. DEENETHORPE.
   USAAF heavy bomber group 1943-45
7. POLEBROOK.
   RAF heavy bombers 1941-42
   USAAF heavy bomber groups 1942-45
8. DESBOROUGH.
   RAF bomber training unit 1943-45
9. GRAFTON UNDERWOOD.
   USAAF heavy bomber groups 1942-45
10. HARRINGTON.
    RAF bomber training unit 1943-44
    USAAF group operating with O.S.S. 1944-45
11. CHELVESTON.
    RAF Central Gunnery School 1941-42
    USAAF heavy bomber groups 1942-45
12. SYWELL.
    RAF elementary pilot training 1939-45
13. DENTON.
    RAF elementary pilot training 1940-45
14. CHIPPING WARDEN.
    RAF bomber training unit 1941-45
15. SILVERSTONE.
    RAF bomber training unit 1943-45
16. HINTON-IN-THE-HEDGES.
    RAF bomber training units 1940-43
    Signals development unit 1943-44
17. CROUGHTON.
    RAF bomber training 1940-42
    RAF pilot training 1943-44
    Glider pilot training 1942-43 and 1944-45

THE END OF THE WAR

283. The V for Victory sign, made famous by Winston Churchill, is much in evidence as happy evacuees return home.

284. Coronation decorations add to the victory spirit in Gladstone Terrace, Northampton.

285. *To them the victory.* The Northamptonshire Regiment receive the Freedom of the County Borough of Northampton, 8th June 1946. The Regiment had fought in many theatres of the war, notably at Dunkirk, in North Africa, Sicily, Italy, North West Europe and Burma.

286. A. V.E. Day street party in The Headlands, Northampton.

287. A V.E. Day street party in Prospect Avenue, Rushden.

288. Workers of E. Parsons & Son Ltd., Irchester, with staff returned from the war. Parsons, in association with Saxby Bros. Ltd., had supplied millions of pork and meat pies (and later in the war packed lunches and jam tarts) in the W.V.S. scheme to provide food for the rural areas; the distribution and sale of the food to some 240 villages was organised for the W.V.S. by Mrs. Gerald Glover of Pytchley House. In 1943 over 5,000,000 pies were sold at a profit of £10,000.

289. Mounts Shoe Factory closing room, Northampton, celebrates on 9th May. Note the bust of Winston Churchill in the foreground.

290. Workers of Wallis and Linnell Ltd., Kettering, celebrate with a victory dance at the Central Hall.

291. A victory bonfire in Sarton's Street, Rushden.

292. Proof positive that the war is over – a serviceman tries on his 'demob' suit.

CHRONOLOGY OF THE SECOND WORLD WAR

1938

29 September. Munich Agreement signed.

1939

15 March. German troops cross Czech frontier.

31 March. Mr. Chamberlain announces British and French guarantees to Poland.

23 August. Soviet-German non-aggression pact signed in Moscow.

1 September. Poland invaded at 5.30 a.m.
Britain and France demand that German troops be withdrawn from Poland.
Official evacuation of children from London and other vulnerable areas of UK begins.

3 September. British ultimatum that German troops be withdrawn from Poland expires 11.00 a.m.; French ultimatum expires 5.0 p.m.
State of war announced.

17 September. Soviet troops enter eastern Poland.

27 September. Warsaw surrenders.

30 November. Finland invaded by Russia.

1940

8 January. Food rationing begins.

12 March. Russo-Finnish peace signed in Moscow.

9 April. German invasion of Denmark and Norway.

10 May. German invasion of Holland, Belgium and Luxembourg.
Resignation of Mr. Chamberlain; coalition government formed with Mr. Churchill as Prime Minister.

14 May. Local Defence Volunteers formed in UK.

15 May. Germans break through across the River Meuse – bridges not destroyed.

28 May. Dunkirk evacuation starts, and continues to the night of 2/3 June. 224,585 British and 112,546 French and Belgian troops evacuated.

29 May. Mr. Bevin, UK Minister of Labour, appeals for 7 day week.

5 June. Battle of France starts.

10 June. Italy declares war on Britain and France from 11 June.

14 June. Germans enter Paris.

10 July. Battle of Britain starts and continues to 31 October.

23 July. LDV renamed 'Home Guard'. Recruiting temporarily suspended as over 1,300,000 have enrolled.

7 September. Opening of London 'Blitz'.

1941

11 March. Lease-lend bill approved, and signed by President Roosevelt.

6 April. Germans invade Greece and Yugoslavia.

10/11 May. Rudolf Hess, Hitler's Deputy, flies from Augsburg to Scotland on private peace mission; lands by parachute near Glasgow.

20 May. Germany invades Crete.

27 May. The *Bismarck* is sunk.

1 June. Clothes rationing starts.

22 June. Germany invades USSR at 4 a.m.

7 December. Japan launches air attack on US naval, military and air bases in Hawaii, including Pearl Harbour.

8 December. USA and UK declare war on Japan.

10 December. HMS *Prince of Wales* and *Repulse* sunk by Japanese air attack off Malayan peninsular.

11 December. Italy and Germany declare war on USA.
USA declares war against both.

25 December. Hong Kong surrenders after 17 day siege.

1942

11/12 February. *Scharnhorst*, *Gneisenau* and *Prinz Eugen* escape from Brest.

12 February. British fail to sink ships, losing 6 Swordfish torpedo planes, 20 bombers and 16 fighters in the attack; enemy losses, 18 fighters.

15 February. Singapore falls.